Interpreting
the Lessons
of the
Church Year

Robin Scroggs

HOLY WEEK

PROCLAMATION 6 | SERIES A

FORTRESS PRESS | MINNEAPOLIS

PROCLAMATION 6
Interpreting the Lessons of the Church Year
Series A, Holy Week

Scripture quotations, unless otherwise noted, are from the New Revised Standard Version Bible, copyright © 1989 by the Division of Christian Education of the National Council of Churches in the U.S.A. and used by permission.

Library of Congress Cataloging-in-Publication Data

Proclamation 6. Series A : interpreting the lessons of the church
  year.
      p. cm.
    Contents: [1] Advent/Christmas / J. Christiaan Beker — [2]
  Epiphany / Susan K. Hedahl — [3] Lent / Peter J. Gomes — [4] Holy
  Week / Robin Scroggs.
    ISBN 0-8006-4207-4 (v. 1 : alk. paper). — ISBN 0-8006-4208-2 (v.
  2 : alk. paper) — ISBN 0-8006-4209-0 (v. 3 : alk. paper) — ISBN 0-8006-4210-4
  (v. 4 : alk. paper)
    1. Bible—Homiletical use. 2. Bible—liturgical lessons,
  English.
  BS534.5P74 1995
  251—dc20   95-4622
                                                            CIP

The paper used in this publication meets the minimum requirements of American National Standard for Information Sciences—Permanence of Paper for Printed Library Materials, ANSI Z329.48-1984. ∞™

Manufactured in U.S.A.   AF 1-4210

99   98   97   96   95   1   2   3   4   5   6   7   8   9   10

Contents

Sunday of the Passion
Palm Sunday

Lectionary	First Lesson	Psalm	Second Lesson	Gospel
Episcopal	Isa. 45:21-25 or Isa. 52:13—53:12	Ps. 22:1-21 or 22:1-11	Phil. 2:5-11	Matt. (26:36-75); 27:1-54 (55-66)
Roman Catholic	Isa. 50:4-7	Ps. 22:8-9, 17-18, 19-20, 23-24	Phil. 2:6-11	Matt. 21:1-11; 26:14—27:66 or 27:11-54
Revised Common	Isa. 50:4-9a	Ps. 31:9-16	Phil. 2:5-11	Matt. 26:14— 27:66 or 27:11-54
Lutheran	Isa. 50:4-9a	Ps. 31:1-5, 9-16	Phil. 2:5-11	Matt. 26:1—27.66 or 27:11-54

FIRST LESSON: ISAIAH 50:4-9A

The readings from the Old Testament for Holy Week focus on the so-called servant songs in 2 Isaiah. The name "2 Isaiah" has been coined to refer to chapters 40–55 in the canonical Isaiah. These chapters are separated from the earlier ones because the majority of this material seems to stem from the late exilic period, written by an unknown prophet whose vision looked forward to the restoration of Israel in Jerusalem.

Within this section scholars have isolated certain portions as the four servant songs, because they seem to have a common theme of a servant who is God's agent in the process of restoration. It must not be forgotten, however, that these remain part of the larger section we name 2 Isaiah, and that in this section God remains deliverer; the servant is just that, the servant of God the Savior.

Just who this enigmatic servant is or was can never be decided. It may have been a historical individual, an idealized individual, a symbol for the collective Israel. Alas, the intense optimism expressed by the prophet was not fulfilled. The Israelites were, indeed, permitted to return, but this and succeeding events did not come close to the dream expressed by 2 Isaiah. Does this mean the servant was a failure? Or that the vision of the prophet was naive and unrealistic?

Traditionally the church has always seen these passages "fulfilled" in Jesus and his death. There is justification for this identification if one focuses on the description in the songs of the *service* required by and offered to God. After all, it is the *quality* of service described here that highlights these songs as distinctive and provocative. The servant, even though or precisely because some royal traits seem to be present, is remarkable because renunciation of the usual means of power is an essential

5

part of the servant's vocation. The description in the Gospels of Jesus' service "fits" the quality of service described in the songs.

The reading for Passion Sunday is the third song (a reading repeated for the Wednesday in Holy Week). Here the quality of service has three dimensions. One is faithful listening (v. 4)—otherwise the service is folly. A second is faithful action (v. 5)—steadfast following of what the servant has heard as God's will. The third is (if necessary) faithful suffering (v. 6)—the willingness to take whatever comes in the way of negative response to faithful proclamation.

Throughout all the passage shines a determined confidence in God—or at least a confidence that the servant knows what God's ways are. This is put in law court imagery in vv. 7-9: "It is the Lord GOD who helps me; who will declare me guilty?" (cf. Rom. 8:31-34). If I am on *God's* side, how can I be defeated? This is dangerously close to the reverse notion, "God's on *my* side." The problem is how to distinguish between the two. The prophet suggests that *listening* is key here; I would add that this means a listening which does not allow one's own ego or anxieties to determine what "God" says. The prophet also suggests that confidence about knowing God's will should be clothed in modesty, even in the face of severe opposition.

PSALM 22:1-24; 31:1-16

These two psalms are similar in type. They both are spoken by a person who suffers greatly, even in danger of death, but who maintains steadfastly trust in God and God's deliverance. The first part of each psalm presents the speaker's distress; at the same time he implores God to save him because of his faithfulness. The speaker's prayer must have been answered, since the second part hymns thanksgiving to God for God's deliverance from near death.

These psalms can rightly be labeled as psalms of the righteous sufferer. While intimately personal in nature, they seem to have a connection with the cult (e.g., 31:25) and were perhaps sung as a thanksgiving for deliverance from dire distress. As a "type" they were transferable from any presumed original situation and made applicable to those who saw themselves in similar plights. Thus it is not surprising that the early church used these psalms explicitly to point to the suffering and deliverance of Jesus (cf. Ps. 31:5 used in Luke 23:46, and the Gospel for Passion Sunday).

SECOND LESSON: PHILIPPIANS 2:5-11

Verses 6-11 are widely recognized as a non-Pauline hymn, the clearest witness to early Christian hymnody in the New Testament. As such it is a crucially important text because the hymn shows what was sung by—and therefore important to—numbers of people of the early church.

It is a hymn about the significance of Jesus, but not the Jesus recognizable in the Gospels. Rather this Jesus is of cosmic scope, a figure whose destiny is to become the ruler of the entire world. If verse 6 refers (as most scholars would affirm) to a state of preexistence, then Jesus moves from preexistence (v. 6) to incarnation (vv. 7-8) to resurrection/exaltation/enthronement (vv. 9-11). If, as some argue, verse 6 is already describing the state of Jesus' humanity, then only two stages are noted in the hymn.

In either case the main content and focus of the hymn is the same. The incarnation of Jesus is not epiphanic (that is, demonstrative of the power of Jesus, as in the Gospels), but hidden. Jesus' life affirms the absolute reality of the tragedy of human existence, all the way to death. Perhaps this reflects a view of the human in which the self is no more than a slave to hostile powers and principalities that rule the cosmos.

The entire action of the hymn is directed to the last three verses, in which Jesus is exalted (the resurrection is assumed but never mentioned) and enthroned (the bestowal of the name is the equivalent to a crowning). All (probably meaning primarily the former "divine" rulers of the world) do obeisance and all confess "*Kyrios Jesus Christos*," "The Lord [of the cosmos] is Jesus Christ." The powers that formerly ruled now must acknowledge, willingly or not, that Jesus Christ has taken their place.

This hymn reveals the audacious faith of the struggling, mostly disenfranchised members of the church, that their hero is not only a *vindicated* executed criminal but has now replaced all rulers in heaven as the rightful sovereign. Nothing is said explicitly about earthly rulers, but there seems little doubt that the enthroned *Kyrios Jesus Christos* is acknowledged as that power which holds sway over all other claims to power, earthly or divine.

Thus Jesus is not just a resurrected individual; he is not just a cultic deity; he is sovereign over the world. Here lies the primary meaning of the resurrection faith for the early church—at least for those who sang these words. The text is actually an ideal text for Easter itself!

There is also an important implication here for Christian ethics. The kind of lord one acknowledges determines the sort of obedience encumbent upon the believer. To submit to a lord who rules the world means to accept duty as servant to that world. Hence, whoever sings this hymn sings his or her commitment to God's world and its problems. Any exegesis that finds the meaning of the hymn simply in Jesus' humility and the call to imitation of such humility tragically misses the point.

GOSPEL: MATTHEW 27:11-54

The Gospel readings for Holy Week are bracketed by the entire story of the last events of Jesus' life as described by Matthew (Passion Sunday) and as described by John (Good Friday). These texts tell a story familiar already to the first hearers of the Gospels, but each Gospel author tells it in a distinctive fashion, to bring out what for the author is the primary *meaning* of the familiar story. On the surface we hear a sad tale of yet another miscarriage of justice. Yet into this seemingly sad tale, our authors weave their interpretations, which provide a meaning of ultimate significance for those of faith.

The large amount of text involved limits me to the task of pointing out to the best of my ability the meaning of the narrative that Matthew has imposed upon the data he has chosen to use. For the homiletical purposes of this volume, such recourse seems most practical and useful. It does mean, however, that we will always be at least once removed from saying that Jesus *actually* did or said such a thing. The reader is invited to consider the exegesis of John in the Good Friday lesson; there I suggest some points of comparison between the two narratives.

The story is terse but highly dramatic. Matthew's readers, just as we ourselves, knew the basic story of Jesus' last day by heart. The hard question then, as now, is whether this terrible execution makes any sense. Assumed is the innocence of Jesus—but innocent people are executed all the time. Is this specific death anything more than yet another example of the travesty of justice in the hands of people whose main motive is to protect their power? And how can there be meaning even if the reader believed that Jesus is God's Messiah? In that case, not only does the death appear to be meaningless suffering; it mocks God.

The most amazing thing about the passion stories in all the Synoptics is how subtly meaning is inserted into the terrible story. Matthew never mitigates (as John sometimes does) the horror of the event. Jesus goes to his death much like all other criminals condemned to death by crucifixion. God does not intervene—indeed, God seems to have disappeared, just as have the disciples. Someone from the inner circle has betrayed him. His fellow Jews, whom he has befriended and aided, demand his death. Nor is any recourse taken to pointers to the resurrection, so that it might suggest: "Just wait a few hours, folks, and it will all be right."

How then do we read the story so that we grasp the meaning Matthew wished to communicate? Several observations may serve to highlight the features of Matthew's story (which are mostly shared with, and may be dependent upon, Mark): (1) Jesus is almost entirely a passive character in the story. Things are done to him; his reaction is not pictured. Indeed, his refusal to defend himself is highlighted by Pilate's amazement. Nothing is said about his physical suffering, although it is assumed throughout. His only spoken line, apart from a terse reply to Pilate (v. 11), is the citation of Psalm 22:1 (v. 46), which, on the surface, is a remarkably strange, indeed horrifying, statement.

(2) The reader is continually confronted with the issue of Jesus' status— "King of the Jews," "Messiah," "King of Israel." Yet it is always the *enemies* that parade these titles, always in a mocking way, because the absurdity of calling a crucified criminal a king is uppermost in their minds (who could fault them?).

This is usually called irony: The mockers speak a truth of which they are not aware. Hence the Roman representative calls Jesus the "King of the Jews" and "Messiah." The Roman soldiers make Jesus "King for a Day" before they kill him. The Jewish leaders deride the titles that believers in Matthew's day accorded Jesus: "King of Israel" and "Son of God" (probably here a synonym for "Messiah"). It is crucial to note, however, that nothing in the text itself feeds such faith. That faith, as far as the Gospel is concerned, arises from previously narrated events.

By definitions accepted in the society of Matthew's day (and ours as well), their mocking is justified. The only way Matthew's readers could buttress their counterclaims is by redefining in a radical way the terms themselves. And that would mean radically redefining the meaning of power.

(3) I think such redefining has, in fact, taken place in the Gospel tradition. In the passion narrative it is introduced into the story by means of the subtle but constant references to the Scriptures (Mark's narrative is primarily responsible for this). Chief among these is Psalm 22, which has influenced the story line itself in a number of places. Jesus' one word from the cross (v. 46) is the clue to the reader that this psalm is key to the meaning of the narrative (the "first footnote" in Christian literature). The dividing of garments (v. 35) and the mocking by the passersby and the Jewish leaders (vv. 39-43) both are dependent upon verses in the psalm. Psalm 69:21 has provided the theme of the offering of drink to Jesus (v. 48). It is also possible that the emphasis upon the silence of Jesus in the hearing before Pilate would suggest to the reader the suffering silence of the servant in Isaiah 53:7 (cf. the first lesson for Good Friday).

These two psalms belong to a category of hymns that can be called the psalm of the righteous, innocent sufferer (cf. the Psalm for Passion Sunday). Through the pointers to this model, the story of Jesus' execution signifies the steadfast, even stubborn (if silent), faith of Jesus: He will remain true to his God no matter what happens. *It is in this faith that lies the true power of the King*. Jesus conquers his foes, because his power is greater than theirs.

Of course this faithful power appears to the world as weakness, so Jesus can be ridiculed and scorned and killed. So enters also the theme of meaning versus meaninglessness. From the perspective of the "wisdom of this world" Jesus' mission and death have no meaning. As Paul comments, it is "foolishness" (cf. 1 Cor. 1:18, 23 and the second lesson for Tuesday of Holy Week). Matthew's story presents not a God who is absent, but one who refuses to play by the world's rules. God is present in the faithfulness of Jesus, and it is this faithfulness that overcomes the apparent meaninglessness of the humiliating death. Looked at in this way, the resurrection of Jesus by God is the way early believers had of expressing their faith in God's power as something totally different from that of a world that knows no other force than brutality and domination. God's power is real; that of the world is sham.

(4) A final motif of the narrative, especially emphasized by Matthew, needs to be thoughtfully considered. This is the tendency, present in all the Gospels, but especially significant in Matthew, to take the "blame" for the execution of the innocent Jesus away from the Romans and place it upon the Jewish leaders. Clearly Jesus was executed by the Romans on a charge that made sense to them (probably insurrection). How they came to that decision cannot be recovered with any assurance, although it does seem likely that some collusion between the Roman and the Jewish authorities occurred.

Why is it, then, that Matthew portrays Pilate as an innocent handwasher, while "all the [Jewish] people" accept responsibility: "His blood be on us and on our children" (v. 25)? The answer lies in the historical situation not of Jesus but of the evangelist, in the later decades of the first century.

After 70 C.E. a gradual and painful separation of church from synagogue began to take place. This separation brought the church more and more under the scrutiny of the Roman authorities, eventually leading to its "status" as an outlaw society.

The hard fact that Jesus was executed by the Romans had to have been a serious obstacle in the emerging Christian struggle for respectability and acceptance in the larger society. To missionize a Jesus legally executed by the Romans as an insurrectionist was fraught with difficulty and danger. The telling of the story had, somehow, to show that Jesus was falsely accused and killed. The Romans had to be shown as innocent. But on whom else to place the blame? The only option was to implicate the Jewish leaders. All of the final forms of the passion stories witness this shift in one way or another.

Matthew seems to go further. He generalizes the responsibility and lays it upon "all the Jews." This is almost certainly a reflection of the bitter antagonism between church and synagogue, visible elsewhere in his Gospel. This was one of the everyday realities of Matthew's church. In my judgment it is best to treat this motif as motivated by people in a seemingly precarious situation. Often people backed against a wall say extreme things. It should not be seen as a divine judgment upon Israel, a view that has had tragic consequences through the succeeding centuries.

The terrible day ends with a quiet note. True, the main intimates of Jesus have fled in fear. But women followers, notably Mary Magdalene, have had the courage to stay and watch, and Joseph of Arimathea, now seen as a disciple of Jesus (so also John 19:38), buries Jesus. But even here nothing hints in the slightest way at the momentous event that will follow. Matthew's story is determined to let the death be present to the reader without providing an escape to the "happy ending." The death has meaning in itself, independent of the resurrection. It might even be said that unless the death carries its own meaning, the resurrection is itself meaningless.

HOMILETICAL REFLECTIONS

These texts plunge us at once and suddenly into what piety describes as the central and most profound mystery of Christianity and what skepticism suspects is the greatest absurdity. One cannot reflect wisely on the provocative meaning of the material without taking seriously both perspectives.

Piety sees here the great lesson of an appropriate humility. The Son of God chooses the way of silent, dutiful suffering. The servant gave his back to those who struck him (Isa. 50:6a). The innocent sufferer in Psalm 22 maintains faith in God through the most abject tortures and mockery. Jesus is, of course, the historical exemplar of this path. Paul adds to the hymn in Philippians the note that the Incarnate One went all the way in servanthood, even to the death of the cross.

The details in Matthew's story are seen by piety to highlight Jesus' humility and powerlessness (which are not necessarily the same thing). One disciple betrays him; another denies him; they all eventually flee, except the women. He is condemned by the authorities of his own people, sentenced to death as a common criminal by the Roman governor. He is mocked by Roman soldiers, taunted by his fellow Jews, railed at even by those suffering with him the horrible death of crucifixion. Through all of this he maintains his silent composure. The reader correctly reads into this account, even if it is not stated explicitly, that Jesus courageously and stubbornly holds to his faith in God and to his seemingly serene conviction that all of this suffering is part of God's plan for the Messiah, the "King of the Jews."

The pious reader knows that this is not the end of the story. On Sunday the tables will be turned. God's Messiah will be resurrected and the path of humility vindicated. Humility, after all, must have its reward, if not immediately, then some day. Because Jesus is God's Son, his reward came immediately. The believer who takes up Jesus' way, Jesus' cross, may have to wait until the resurrection at the last day.

The *skeptic* hears the story in significantly different ways. He may, of course, superficially reject any suffering or commitment unless it is forced upon him, and then he can only feel it as meaninglessness. But there are much more serious objections by skeptics that believers need to ponder.

One comes from Nietzsche, who cries "ressentiment, ressentiment." While he had a remarkably positive view of Jesus' death ("There was only one Christian and he died on the cross"), Nietzsche sees the believer's exaltation of humility as an attempt to hide his powerlessness. What you can't have, you are not supposed to have. That such justification is potentially present in Christian talk about humility needs to be acknowledged. One could even wonder if the word *humility* should be abandoned. Perhaps only she who doesn't know she is humble can be genuinely humble.

Another skeptic's reaction takes the issues of commitment and the necessity of suffering seriously but asks, "Why is Jesus' example unique and thus worthy of especial note?" Countless others have suffered and died for causes, have been equally committed and steadfast in the face of oppressive enemies. That Jesus believed in his cause does not separate him from the others. And the more one wants to think that Jesus knew God would resurrect him, the less remarkable Jesus' commitment becomes. Just this happens in John's story of the passion, summarized clearly in Jesus' claim earlier in the narrative: "I have power to lay it [my life] down, and I have power to take it up again" (John 10:18). In this view, any claim for the uniqueness of Jesus' suffering is misguided.

A final skepticism can be voiced about the validity of one's commitment itself. Just as history has exampled many stories of courageous commitment to causes, so it knows many cases of tragic delusion. How does one know that one's cause is "true" and worthy of that serious commitment that will accept suffering and death? If we take Jesus' humanity seriously, how did *he* "know" that his commitment was worth it?

I suggest that we can only plumb the depths of the Christian story if we take the skeptics seriously. It is crucial to burst the balloon of superficial piety. The story of Jesus' passion and the believer's involvement in it inevitably thrust one into the ambiguity of one's commitment precisely at the point where one cries out: "Is my faith worth the cost?" If my cause is based on psychological need, if it is rooted in something less than "ultimate," if it is even folly, then are not the mockers correct?

True faith can occur only at the point where the ambiguity is recognized; decision can only mean something if it is taken knowing that it could be wrong. Cost is not cost unless one is aware that one may be paying too much. *The decision is a wager that the world is wrong in its rules about power.* To set aside those rules and abide by those claimed by the story of Jesus to be the *real* rules because they are God's is to be as virtually alone as Jesus was on Golgotha.

It is helpful here to see that Matthew's story, even if the author and reader know that resurrection follows, does not try to avoid the ambiguity of Jesus' death. Nor do the texts about the servant and the righteous sufferer "prove" that the heroes are correct. In all cases we have commitment over against the majority opinion, which seems to win out. Who is to say which is correct?

After all, what does "winning" prove? It means something only measured by some set of rules. But what if the rules change? According to the rules of power set by the world, Jesus loses. But what if Jesus is playing by a different set of rules, where power means something radically different? Suppose power for Matthew's Jesus is the power that serves rather than dominates (cf. 20:28)? Then who wins?

Monday in Holy Week

Lectionary	First Lesson	Psalm	Second Lesson	Gospel
Episcopal	Isa. 42:1-9	Ps. 36:5-10	Heb. 9:39—12:3	John 12:1-11 or Mark 14:3-9
Roman Catholic	Isa. 42:1-7	Ps. 27:1-3, 13-14		John 12:1-11
Revised Common	Isa. 42:1-9	Ps. 36:5-11	Heb. 9:11-15	John 12:1-11
Lutheran	Isa. 42:1-9	Ps. 36:5-10	Heb. 9:11-15	John 12:1-11

FIRST LESSON: ISAIAH 42:1-9

The Old Testament lectionary now turns back to the so-called first servant song, although scholars tend to see verses 1-4 and 5-9 as originally separate songs. Its interpretation depends in part on the identity of the servant, but we have already seen that it is impossible to determine with any assurance who the servant is. I will continue to focus on the *service* spoken of rather than the *servant*.

In this passage the servant has royal functions and power and is so designated and presented by Yahweh himself: "Here is my servant . . . my chosen . . . I have put my spirit upon him" (v. 1). Similar presentations can be found in Psalms 2 and 110. His primary task is to bring *mishpat* (v. 1d). This word can be variously translated as "judgment," "justice," or "verdict." It is, by implication, God's own judgment or justice, and the service of the servant lies precisely in acting out God's decisions.

Furthermore (and similar to royal hyperbole elsewhere, e.g., Ps. 2:8-11), this judgment is not to be just for or on Israel, but on "the earth," the "coastlands" (v. 4); he is "a light to the nations" (v. 6). This judgment will be something "new," not just a repetition of the past (v. 9).

Precisely because the servant here is described with a royal function, the *means* by which this activity is to be carried out is remarkable. The servant will not exercise his power by the usual domineering force of a tyrant, who decrees that people will be subjected to him. "He will not cry or lift up his voice . . . a bruised reed he will not break, and a dimly burning wick he will not quench" (vv. 2-3)—exquisite images for gentleness and sensitivity. He also will free the captives; here the reference may be to the expected liberation of Israelite prisoners in the Exile.

Whether the servant in this song is a historical individual (perhaps even Cyrus?) or not, the royal activity of nondominating gentleness is certainly idealized. It is this idealization of gentleness that distinguishes this passage from other royal idealizations of domination over the earth. Here is a vision of a different form of power that, instead of causing the usual cowering before a tyrant's force, will lead to people waiting (positively) for his instruction (v. 4). The grandeur of the passage lies just in this reversal of the understanding of power, a claim that there is a strength in gentleness which is greater and ultimately more effective than the power of domination, the only meaning of power known by the world.

This service is not, however, independent of God. In fact, it is set between the acknowledgment of the creative activity in the past of God (v. 5) and God's own affirmation that new things are about to happen (v. 9). The activity of the servant is at the cutting edge of the future—"Before they [new events] spring forth, I tell you of them." The proclamation by the servant and his gentle but effective rulership belong to God's ongoing design to realize God's intent in creation.

PSALM 36:5-11

Psalm 36 divides itself into three parts. Part 1 (vv. 1-4) is a Wisdom-like passage attacking the "wicked." Part 2 (vv. 5-10) is a hymn of praise to God for the covenant mercies shown the righteous. Part 3 (vv. 11-12) returns to the theme of the wicked, now in direct relationship to the psalmist.

The situation reflected may be that of a person who, beset by powerful enemies, has sought asylum in the temple (vv. 7-8). Safe in the temple, he praises the covenant loyalty of God (vv. 5-6). He piles up the terms that characterize God's covenant fidelity—"steadfast love," "faithfulness," "righteousness," and "judgments." The covenant extends to the animal world as well as to Israel (6c).

In verses 7-9 the psalmist describes the joy of being present in the temple, the sacrificial meals (v. 8) and other cultic activities (v. 9). In verses 10-11 he prays that God will show his covenant fidelity by continuing to bless those who cling to God and by protecting him from the wicked. This psalm affords an interesting glimpse into a social function the temple had. It could serve to protect from enemies a person who was not able to defend him- or herself in the outside world.

SECOND LESSON: HEBREWS 9:11-15

Three of the epistle readings for Holy Week, including that for Monday, are taken from Hebrews, the most difficult and to modern minds most obscure writing in the New Testament. This is due to the central metaphor the author has chosen, namely, that of the priestly, sacrificial cultus. If all theology is metaphorical—and a good argument can be made for that assertion—then clarity of communication depends upon the selection of the root metaphor to be used. Our Western world is so estranged from sacrificial practices that Hebrews comes close to making little sense to us.

The *first* step toward understanding is to recognize the pervasive sacrificial language of Hebrews as a giant metaphor. The language is not used literally. The author is not, for example, talking about the "real" blood of Jesus. He creates elaborate parallels and counterparallels between the sacrificial cult and the activity of Jesus. Jesus is a high priest, who enters into the heavenly temple (as a result of his resurrection), offering himself as a sacrifice! Taken literally, the image borders on the bizarre; the point is that at each turn there is an analogy drawn with the earthly cultus. Of course, for our author the act of Jesus is "how much more" effective to achieve its desired purpose.

But what is the desired purpose? The *second* step toward understanding is to ask *why* an author chooses such metaphor(s) and what an author accomplishes by the use of the chosen metaphor that would not so easily be reached by the choice of another one. Paul, for example, chooses a legal metaphor (justification) as his central language, in part, no doubt, because of his legal training. Another way of putting the question is to ask what *problem* the author thinks to address by the metaphor of choice.

In our passage (which tersely summarizes much of the conceptual framework of the author) we can, I think, find some indications of the problem he perceives to be crucial and how his interpretation of the act of Christ addresses the problem. The death/resurrection of Christ is an unrepeatable event that results in an *eternal* (i.e., valid for all time) redemption (v. 12). The key sentence in the entire passage is the expression of the result of Jesus' act: It "purifies our conscience from dead works to worship the living God" (v. 14). Exegesis must thus focus on the meaning of this sentence.

What problem shimmers through this language? It may seem banal to say that the problem is sin, but that is where the author begins (it is not the only or even most prominent problem perceived by New Testament authors!). What is it about sin that troubles him, in view of the fact that the Jewish cultus has a complete and elaborate procedure for dealing with it? He perceives in the necessarily repeated and, to him, partial results of the cultus a serious inadequacy. What he wants is a permanently effective event ("an eternal redemption"). But in what sense is it to be effective?

In the ancient world "conscience" did not point to an innate agency of the self that monitored possible future acts. It meant, rather, the mental acknowledgment that what one had done in the past was either right or wrong. It is this activity of inspection of the past that he wants to "purify." The cultic activity of purification is unusual as applied to mental activities such as conscience and is used only here in Hebrews. But "to purify the conscience" must mean to enable the mind to be free from lasting negative assessments about past activities (this must be what is meant by the phrase, "dead works").

This would not mean that the mind could say, "What I did wasn't so bad after all." It would mean, rather, "The guilt that has been festering because of what I did that was wrong has been taken away." The consuming anxiety that keeps me from living in the present ("to worship the living God") has dissipated, and *I am free from the past*. While it may appear anachronistic to say that the author is troubled by the subjective awareness of guilt, that may indeed be what he thinks is abolished by the once-for-all "sacrifice" of Jesus.

The death/resurrection of Jesus means release from the past so that one can focus on the present in full joy to serve "the living God" (v. 14), to be free to live in "the good things that have come" (v. 11), to be able fully to consider oneself to be a recipient of the promise of the eternal inheritance (v. 15).

We can rejoice that the author has come to this awareness of present freedom from the guilt brought by sin. He has come to this self-understanding through Christianity and he calls us to the same liberation. This does not mean that we are bound to his metaphor. Nor does it necessitate the rejection of sacrificial metaphors that others have found meaningful in a way he did not.

GOSPEL: JOHN 12:1-11

Some version of this story, an anointing of Jesus by a woman, was obviously popular and important in the earliest church. There are three canonical versions of it, Mark 14:3-9 (par. Matt. 26:6-13), Luke 7:36-50, and our Johannine passage. Motifs and details overlap and intertwine so that it is largely guesswork as to which version is earlier or more "authentic." It is best to stay with our Johannine text and insert that into the plot of the Gospel as a whole. What does John want us to hear in this account?

The story itself is straightforward, even if its meaning is not. Jesus is being honored at a formal meal, in which the participants (normally males only) are reclining, leaning on one elbow, so that they face the platform on which the food is placed and their legs and feet extend away from the platform. The women (here Martha is named) are serving. Mary (just as the unnamed woman in Luke 7) goes to the feet of Jesus and anoints them with an extravagantly expensive perfume worth 300 denarii. A denarius was typically said to be a day's wages for a laborer; hence the perfume was equal in value to a year's pay for a poor Jewish family. She wipes the perfume off with her hair (a detail similar to that in Luke, where it makes better sense than here), and the fragrance permeates the house.

At this point evil Judas begins the dialogue with Jesus, a dialogue that is similar to that in the Markan story, apart from the bad motives assigned to the speaker. As in Mark the conflict is about the proper use of limited resources. This extravagant expense should have been channeled to the needy rather than being needlessly wasted on a (liturgical?) act of homage. Jesus rejects this statement of priorities and suggests that the act, symbolizing in some way his death and burial, is appropriate. He ends the discussion with a logion (clearly the form of the narrative is basically a pronouncement story) that distinguishes what is an appropriate usual expenditure for the poor from this extraordinary symbolic act.

Typical of the function of a pronouncement story, the narrative deals with tension within the communities who told it about the best use of the churches' monies. This is as true of the Markan version as here, and it is a tension that has ever since been present within Christianity. Presumably the early communities were not wealthy, its members largely from the peasant or urban underclass, and the use of a year's pay for an act of homage, even to Jesus, seen by some as a callous neglect of the needs of people.

Since many in the church today would agree with the priority here assigned to Judas, Jesus' reply is as provocative today as then. His response walks a tightrope. Use of resources to care for the needy is proper ("You always have the poor with you"), but singular acts of homage to the Lord of the church sometimes take precedence ("You do not always have me"). Is this an appropriate balance? The issue was debated then and will always be.

John puts the story within his own plot, and cognizance of this location adds to our understanding of the meaning of the narrative for the Gospel. It occurs immediately after the key scene of the raising of Lazarus. The *dramatis personae* of that scene are participants now in the anointing story. The author has made it clear that Jesus' act of raising Lazarus to life will result in Jesus being condemned to death (11:45-53), and appended to the anointing story itself is the chilling announcement that that resurrection will also result in the death of Lazarus (vv. 10-11). Thus the stories are closely intertwined. Jesus' act for Lazarus will result in the death of both, and Lazarus's sister performs the first act of preparation for Jesus' death. Themes of life and death are thus inextricably related.

The act of anointing precedes the triumphal entry, where the crowds gather to proclaim the kingship of Jesus (12:12-15). Some thus see the anointing as one of royalty. If so, however, it is ironic: The anointing is for the death of the king. The king, apparently, does *not* live forever.

Perhaps more obvious is the link between the anointing of the feet and the washing by Jesus of the disciples' feet in the final dinner (13:1-20; cf. the Gospel for Maundy Thursday). Before Jesus performs his act of service, the woman has acted out hers. In both instances, the act is more than an act of service; but in both instances it is *also* service, explicitly in the case of Jesus' act (cf. 13:12-16), and implicitly in Mary's act (more explicitly stated in Mark's version—14:9).

HOMILETICAL REFLECTIONS

The themes of service and its corollary, the reversal of the understanding of power, permeate the texts for Holy Week. Ultimately they coincide. True service lies in acts of self-giving that are the opposite of domineering force. The relation between the two is, however, tricky. Does one perform an act of self-giving *so that* one may exercise power? To do that would insidiously reverse the priority our texts assign, but it must be acknowledged that the temptation to do this can and does happen, especially, perhaps, within the church where the ideal of self-giving is so strongly enshrined.

Self-giving can exercise a powerful control over the recipient, as all who feel "in debt" to another person can acknowledge. That is, self-giving can function as a subtle but no less domineering force over others. When that happens self-giving is no longer true giving and has become domination concealed behind an ideal. Surely the church needs to hear this! Pious ministers and laypeople become dominating, and there seems little self-awareness of this domination precisely because it is hidden behind the ideal of service. "I have served you, so be grateful!" And we all have experienced the frustration of trying to get behind that protective mask when we must deal with people who use it.

The way out of this impasse is not easy. The ideal of service is too centrally located in Christianity to give that up. And it is inevitably the way of the world to seek power to control and thus preserve or better one's place in it. Two things can be said, but they are "hard sayings." The first is that true service means single-mindedness toward the needs of the one being served. If other considerations enter the motivation of the server, then it is not true service.

But how can other considerations *not* enter? How can a Christian avoid the seemingly inevitable need to protect one's place and what better way to do so than to hide it behind an appeal to service? This leads to the second issue: One must be so convinced that *God* protects one that the need to protect oneself does not enter the act of service. Our texts for Holy Week do not deal with that theme (except the epistle reading of 1 Corinthians 1; cf. the second lesson for Tuesday in Holy Week), but, in my judgment, it is basic to any realistic discussion about keeping service from becoming self-serving. This is the awareness that is trumpeted by Paul: Justification by grace means that life is sheer gift; *thus need for power and domination does not exist* and true caring for the neighbor becomes for the first time possible. Only the person who can completely forget the self can completely care for the self of another.

The Gospel text raises a second difficulty for Christians in relation to the service of giving. What sort of priorities are appropriate for giving from limited resources? The woman gave extravagantly, yes, but she gave for a purpose that had no result in the physical improvement of her friends— or even, one could argue, in the spiritual. The countersuggestion, this extravagance should better have been spent on the poor, sounds right; yet it is rejected by Jesus' response.

This issue continues to haunt us. Was the splendor of the medieval cathedrals erected at the cost of the physical improvement of the towns-people? How do we justify today grand architectural designs, elaborate music programs, expensive preachers while people starve and are homeless? Even to suggest that there is a real issue is a bold statement for some today.

Does Jesus' word have anything to commend it? It is hard for me to doubt that behind this story lies some liturgical scene in the early church (cf. especially Mark 14:9). At any rate, let's imagine such a possibility. In the liturgical drama that takes place yearly at the memorial of Jesus' death, some community has symbolized the burial of Jesus by the use of ointments. That symbolization has become meaningful, expressing the group's participation in the sorrow and significance of its master's death. Perhaps some member of the community provides the ointment for the liturgical act.

But the community is not on the whole wealthy; at least some of its members are poor and needy. Some of them think their needs should take precedence over the beauty of the act (remember: its fragrance filled the room!). Some of the wealthier members take that view as well, feeling righteous indignation about the "wastefulness" of the symbolism. Whose side would we have been on?

Is beauty and power that captures religious reality of no importance when put beside physical well-being? Is an essential part of the life of a believer the moments of exalted experience provoked by a beautiful build-ing, well-performed music, inspired preaching? Or is it needless expense that could be avoided if Christians were truly committed?

On the other hand, is the focus on physical well-being as the *central* task of Christianity a sellout to materialism? Is it not the case that the poor have a sense of the need for the spiritual as well as the physical in their lives? Do the poor need inspired preaching any less than the wealthy? Or is such defense of the legitimacy of "expensive ointments" a protective device to shield one from responsibility?

I do not think there is a pat answer—nor does the Gospel story provide one. The story says that at some key moments "expensive ointments" are appropriate, without either listing the criteria for such moments or ignoring that the needs of the poor are real. As so often happens, the biblical text raises issues without providing our own times with easy answers.

Tuesday in Holy Week

Lectionary	First Lesson	Psalm	Second Lesson	Gospel
Episcopal	Isa. 49:1-6	Ps. 71:1-12	I Cor. 1:18-31	John 12:37-38, 42-50 *or* Mark 11:15-19
Roman Catholic	Isa. 49:1-6	Ps. 71:1-6, 15, 17		John 13:21-23, 36-38
Revised Common	Isa. 49:1-7	Ps. 71:1-14	I Cor. 1:18-31	John 12:20-36
Lutheran	Isa. 49:1-6	Ps. 71:1-12	I Cor. 1:18-25	John 12:20-36

FIRST LESSON: ISAIAH 49:1-7

This is the second servant song. According to most scholars it ends after verse 6. The speaker addresses his hearers and reports what Yahweh has and will do through him. The vision is staggering!

He is called as a servant—but what kind? Verse 1 reverberates with the call speech of Jeremiah (Jer. 1:5). It would seem that the call is to be a prophet, yet other motifs are present which obscure a simple identification. In verse 2 the images of sword and arrow are used, on the literal level referring to a warring figure, perhaps a king. Since, however, these are images, and it is the servant's *speech* that is the literal "sword," it is likely that the prophetic function of the prophet is the referent. In verse 3, it is clearly the collective "Israel" who is the servant. In this case we are not dealing with an individual at all; rather, the point of the language is to refer to the mission of an entire people, languaged in prophetic imagery.

Since (to complicate the matter further) the servant in verse 5 *is* separate from the collective Jacob and Israel, it perhaps makes the most sense to take the entire passage as referring to an individual figure and to assume that the word *servant* in verse 3 was added after the text was composed. If so, however, it is a very early gloss; the Isaiah scroll from the Dead Sea includes the word and it is presupposed in the text used by the Greek translator(s) of the Septuagint, sometime before the common era.

The ambiguity about the identity of the servant suggests again that it is best to focus on the mission to which the servant feels called. And that is daunting and audacious enough! Through the servant God will be glorified, that is, revealed, made known (cf. the Gospel for today).

That task seems impossible to the speaker; in verse 4 he points to his sense of futility in his work, despite his devotion to God. God seems to have little sympathy with this self-pity (a typical divine reaction to prophets!) and reminds him of his mission to Israel and Jacob. What this mission is to result in is not certain—to "restore" could have political meaning. Is the mission to enable Israel and Jacob to regain political independence? Or does it have primarily a religious tone? Whatever the nuance, God pointedly suggests that the already assigned task, which has seemed to the servant too impossible as it is, is not enough! More! More! The servant is now to be "a light to the nations/Gentiles," the agent of God's "salvation" to "the end of the earth/land." The question is the meaning of these phrases. "Salvation" must be seen as deliverance from evil, distress—political, military, natural. It cannot have the sense that it has come to have in Christianity—forgiveness of sins or the bestowal of eternal life. Thus "a light to the nations" must be taken in this context. Just as the servant will deliver Israel and Jacob from distress, so he is called to do this to other peoples as well. Given the political/military situation at the time of 2 Isaiah—the emergence of the power of Persia (seen by the prophet as positive—as "salvation"), it may suggest that the mission of the prophet is in line with the political program of the new Persian power.

How the servant is to accomplish such "salvation" is not specified. Is he somehow to do it himself? Is he simply announcing what Yahweh is going to do? Is he announcing what he thinks Persia is to do? None of this is clear. Obviously the servant must have had some strategy in mind. What we can know is that the servant acknowledges a claim on his loyalty which pushes him beyond narrow and safe territories, which calls him to an activity that seems beyond his powers to realize. The implication seems to be that the divine claim silences his lack of confidence, his "realistic" appraisal of what is possible. He must take up what he sees as God's task, having little to go on except the sense that "My God has become my strength" (v. 5).

Verse 7, presumably the beginning of a following section, certainly speaks of the servant, here characterized as despised and abhorred by the nations. The verse is a promise of ultimate exaltation because of the victory of the faithful God. God has chosen the servant, and God will stand with him throughout the seemingly impossible mission.

PSALM 71:1-17

This psalm belongs also to the category of the innocent sufferer. The speaker also perhaps has sought asylum in the temple (v. 3; cf. the Psalm for Monday in Holy Week). What sets off this psalm from the others is its explicit note that the singer is an old man. This means, on the one hand, that he can appeal to a lifelong devotion to God (vv. 6, 17). On the other, his enemies think he is easy prey because he is old and, for some reason, is considered forsaken by God (vv. 11, 18). The singer intersperses pleas for deliverance (and deserved punishment on his enemies) and praises to God.

The man's plight is intensified because he has no one to aid him in his fight with his enemies (v. 11b). Perhaps he has outlived his family, or they have also deserted him. Thus he has little resort but to take to the temple and seek refuge in God (which includes the protection the temple offers!).

SECOND LESSON: I CORINTHIANS 1:18-31

This famous passage is perhaps the classic example of Paul's vision of a new world based on an understanding of reality and power that is opposite to that of the "world." "World" here must be seen as any social construction of reality accepted as true by the various sociopolitical systems of the ancient world (and ours as well), systems that Paul characterizes as "Jew" and "Greek."

These systems base their respective understandings on power (the Jews seek signs; i.e., miracles) and human wisdom (Greek). Against these Paul posits the act of God in Christ, which creates a new and, for him, true world based on the cross—that is, ultimately, on the self-giving power of God, which is at the same time an expression of true wisdom.

This passage is falsely interpreted if one reads into it a view of God's reality based on weakness and foolishness. That is, it is not a masochistic view of the world. It is only by the false perspectives of human notions of power and wisdom that the new world created by the cross is judged to be weakness and foolishness. In the cross, rather, is revealed what power and wisdom are all about. "For God's foolishness is wiser than human wisdom, and God's weakness is stronger than human strength" (v. 25).

What then *is* the cross? On the surface it is the ultimate sign of human degradation and weakness—a person executed by political authority as a criminal, dying a slow and agonizing death. How can Paul then claim it to be the opposite—a revelation of God's power and wisdom? Alas, Paul does not explain here or elsewhere in any satisfying manner.

Yet the general direction of Paul's thinking is clear from his overall interpretation of God's act. The cross, just because it is the ultimate sign of suffering, reveals a God who, in the offering of the son, is willing to give Herself selflessly and completely ("did not withhold his own Son"—Rom. 8:32). The cross has the power to "reconcile the world" (2 Cor. 5:19), that is, to overcome human hostility against a God who has been falsely perceived as the unyielding Father (Rom. 5:10).

In the cross God is revealed as one who gives, not God as a righteous judge who accepts or condemns on the basis of command. God *is* righteous and *is* judge, but the first word about God is about the gracious power that accepts (justifies) all humans even though they are sinners. They are sinners precisely because they live in the false world based on a false belief in God (cf. Rom. 1:18 25). The cross is thus the decisive revelation of the reality of God, and the God it reveals is a God whose power is love and whose wisdom is to go to whatever lengths it takes to reconcile humanity to Herself.

Paul is not, however, speaking of a kind of forgiveness that leaves sinners where they are. The proclamation of the cross is that revelatory event which *empowers* one to "switch worlds," to leave that world based on a God who symbolizes human propensity to grasp after power and control. It frees one to enter a new world based on a radically giving God, who now symbolizes what true power and wisdom are.

To live in this new world not only changes one's view of oneself, it also alters how one relates to others. This new relationship is, in fact, the reason Paul says what he does in our passage. Divisiveness is present in the Corinthian community, and Paul reads this situation as caused by appeals to human understandings of power (my leader is better than yours!) and wisdom (I've got a better theology than you do!). He calls them back to basics, to realize once again that they now live in a different world, a world in which interpersonal relationships come from the perception that all one has is gift. The gifted is now free to acknowledge others' gifts.

Thus in verses 26-31 he turns to speak about the healing of the tensions. To base one's life on human values (i.e., that of the false world) is ridiculous—even by such standards not many have legs to stand on. The true *basis* for relationships is the constant confidence that everything one is is gift from God. No one can boast in herself and thus claim superiority over others.

The true *quality* of relationship in this new world is the same self-forgetfulness about status and authority that God exhibited in the cross. One could appeal here to Paul's description of the transformed person in the list of virtues in Galatians 5:22-23: "The fruit of the Spirit is love, joy, peace, patience, kindness, generosity, faithfulness, gentleness, and self-control." This is the self one brings to interpersonal relationships, a self based on confidence in God and thus free from that anxiety which needs to control and dominate.

Hence one cannot boast in oneself. True boasting is in God, that is, in the awareness that life is gift from God, a gift to be shared in one's caring relationships with others. For Paul the solution to problems in relationships is not to try harder to be perfect; it is, rather, to recall for oneself the very basis of Christian existence.

GOSPEL: JOHN 12:20-50

It is widely recognized that the Gospel of John is intentionally structured by its author so that there are two or three distinct sections or "books." Book One ends with chapter 12 and contains Jesus' confrontation with "the world" or "the Jews." Book Two begins with chapter 13 and includes Jesus' message to his disciples, that is, the church. If one wishes to separate the story of the passion and resurrection, then Book Three begins at chapter 18.

The reading for today for most of the liturgical traditions contains the climax of Book One. Here the meaning of the death is revealed (vv. 20-36a), and the author writes his final words of this Book, in part put into his own direct comment (vv. 36b-43), in part through a final speech of Jesus (vv. 44-50).

The material here is profound and provocative and yet extremely difficult, since there is little in the way of logical progression of ideas. It is best to proceed in a verse-by-verse interpretation.

Verses 20-22.   Greeks attending the Passover festival appear and as abruptly disappear. Given the larger context they must be Gentiles and must symbolize their incorporation into the church. The brief narrative deals with an issue frequently expressed in the New Testament—namely, the appropriateness and timing of Gentiles entering an originally Jewish movement. Matthew places the inclusion in the resurrected Jesus' command (28:16-20) and Luke at the event of Peter's baptism of Cornelius in Acts 10. It is likely that Mark ascribes the inclusion to the actual ministry of Jesus at the second feeding story (8:1-13). For John the incorporation is tied to the death of Jesus. Clearly this attention in the narratives indicates that the entry of Gentiles, and the conditions for their entry, was a matter of concern not only in Paul's environment.

The Greeks seek out Philip, a Greek-named disciple from a mixed Gentile/Jewish region in Galilee, and request to "see Jesus." This seemingly innocent word, *see,* is loaded with symbolism in John. In the Gospel it denotes coming to true faith in God. For John, "Whoever has seen me has seen the Father" (14:9). In this case the banal statement "Seeing is believing" is true.

Verse 23.   "The hour has come for the Son of Man to be glorified." The "hour" is the eschatological event, not simply of the death but of the resurrection as well. Up to this point the "hour" had not yet come (2:4, 7:30, 8:20). The desire of the Gentiles to come to faith signifies to Jesus that his hour has indeed come.

The *meaning* of the "hour" is the glorification of the Son of Man. In this Gospel the title *Son of Man* points to Jesus as the medium of revelation between the transcendent and the immanent, between God and this world. "Glory" has for John its Old Testament significance, the "revelation of God." Thus the glorification of Jesus means the revelation of God—this is key to understanding the section as a whole (although the connection will not explicitly be made until vv. 28-30). *The entire mission of Jesus is to reveal the reality of God.* The glorification of Jesus is not *self-glorification*; indeed, for Jesus it means his death. Yet the author believes that it is in the death that the reality of God is most clearly "seen." What does this mean? The passage never says explicitly, but the implication in the next verses points in the direction of the author's intent.

Verses 24-26. Verse 24 points directly to Jesus' death as the meaning of the glorification, and the death here is seen as giving and service. Its purpose is to "bear fruit" (cf. also 13:31-35). What is remarkable is that in both this passage and 13:31-35 the thought slips almost immediately to the call to service of the disciples, to "follow" Jesus in his self-giving love. The issue seems to be not some abstract theologizing, but its practical application in the church, its "fruit."

The author uses traditional sayings to make his point (cf., e.g., Mark 8:34-35). He probably chose them because they link discipleship to the self-giving of Jesus on the cross. The Christology of John certainly contains much more than that of example (unless one would say that Jesus imitates the Father and so follows God's "example"). But it is *also* example—and participation. The one who obeys Jesus' word is "in" the divine reality, which is salvatory existence (14:23).

Verse 27. Here is an oblique, but clear, allusion to the Gethsemane story of the Synoptics—a story John does not choose to narrate. What is remarkable is that John places the scene in an entirely different context; Jesus' word is spoken in the presence of the "world." It is in effect a rejection of the mood of the traditional story. When Jesus does pray to God at the last night, it is a speech full of confidence in the success of God's overarching plan for humanity.

Verses 28-30. Now Jesus explains that the "hour" means the glorification of the reality of God. A divine voice confirms the correctness of Jesus' statement, the future tense probably referring to the resurrection event still to come. The "crowd," as so often in the Gospel, does not grasp what is being said. This is emphasized by the double interpretations suggested. Verse 30 is confusing, but perhaps indicates that God has provided the resources for true understanding, resources that the crowd has ignored.

Verses 31-33. The meaning of the hour is now further explained. As the eschatological event it means the end of the evil power over the world (a typical motif in apocalyptic) and its opposite, salvatory, result—the elevating of "all" into the reality of the divine. These are not, however, in John's revisioning of Jewish eschatology, future events; they are present realities, present in the revelation of the "hour" and present to those who "see." That John means here a "universal salvation" is unlikely in view of many other passages. It is universal only in the sense that Gentiles as well as Jews are now participants in salvation. The "lifting up from the earth" (cf. also 3:13-15) is a triple *entendre*, referring at the same time to (1) the crucifixion, (2) the resurrection, and (3) the return to the transcendent realm from which he originally came. Salvador Dalí's *Crucifixion* catches the meaning of this passage in an arresting way.

Verses 34-36a. This is perhaps the strangest part of the scene, full of non sequiturs. The "crowd" does not understand, retorts that its understanding is that the salvatory agent (here named as *Christos*) does not go away. What is the meaning of the departure of the Son of Man, whoever that is? To reintroduce the Son of Man into the discussion the crowd would have to have remembered Jesus' statement in verse 23. The reader, of course, will be aware of what the term means and will perhaps have remembered that in 3:13-15 Jesus speaks of the lifting up in terms of that title.

Jesus seemingly ignores the crowd's perplexity and addresses not the meaning of the departure but the urgent moment, the need to come to faith now while the departure is "not yet." His language is couched in the image of light/darkness and has a humorous touch to it: the image of the bumbling, fumbling person who is trying to find his/her way in the midst of complete darkness. In our mostly urban setting, where there is rarely any real darkness, we have to think our way back into a time when outside the shine of murky lamps and the moon, the darkness can be disabling, even frightening. At any rate, his final request is urgently serious: Become "children of light."

With that final thrust, Jesus closes his debate with the "world," although at the trial Jesus will enter into dialogue with Pilate. The author, however, is not ready to conclude Book One and adds two additional sections. The first acknowledges and "explains" the failure of the Johannine church in its mission. The second gives Jesus the final word as he stands alone "on stage."

It is widely recognized that the history of the Johannine community reflected in the Gospel is one of Jewish believers in Jesus who eventually found it impossible to remain within the bounds of the synagogue. This was due, apparently, to the increasingly sharp divide between the two communities over views about Jesus. From the standpoint of the synagogue the Johannine church had overstepped, in its ascriptions to Jesus, appropriate limitations about human mediatorial figures. The Johannine community, the synagogue claimed, had made Jesus into a "second god" (cf.

5:18). One weapon in the hands of the synagogue leaders (in the Gospel pointed to by the "Pharisees") was to debar members who insisted in making such extravagant claims. What sort of "excommunication" this may have been is not certain, but the implication, it seems to me, is that it is permanent. The word used by the Gospel is, literally, "out-synagogue" (9:22; 12:42; 16:2), a term apparently coined by the community to translate some Hebrew or Aramaic formula. This history serves to explain the two final sections of Book One.

Verses 36b-43. Jesus' mission has failed. Since in the story of Jesus the story of the Johannine church is mirrored, what is being said is that the Johannine church's mission has failed. Instead of convincing its co-religionists that they should believe in Jesus, the synagogue has drawn the line and begun to exclude believers in Jesus who insisted in making claims about the "divinity" of Jesus. (This does not mean that it excluded *any* member who honored Jesus.)

The failure must have been so apparent to both the church and its enemies that it cried out for explanation. The author decides to confront it at this point in the plot, probably because it "fits" the story but also perhaps because it provided a look ahead to the rejection of Jesus in the passion account. If Jesus' teaching is rejected, then it is not surprising that his coreligionists will conspire against him later.

The author finds it convenient to appeal to Scripture to "explain" the failure. The passages of Isaiah used here were also chosen by other Christians to explain just what John has to explain. Isaiah 53:1 is used for the same purpose by Paul in Romans 10:16. Isaiah 6:10 is cited by Mark (4:12) and the author of Acts (28:26-27). John also appeals, however, to believers who remained within the synagogue although they "secretly" believed in Jesus. This must reflect the historical situation and shows that there was a more fluid relationship between church and synagogue than the author of the Gospel thinks is appropriate.

Verses 44-50. Jesus, seemingly speaking to no one, has the final word. On the surface this final word is a pastiche of previous statements by Jesus. Thus it serves as a kind of summary of his teaching. The summary has, nevertheless, a particular direction. All of the statements serve to deflect attention from the person of Jesus, while at the same time not denying his centrality. The basic message is that Jesus is "simply" the window through which God appears. Salvation and judgment are embedded in Jesus' activity, but the true actors are God, on the one hand, and Jesus' teaching, on the other. "On the last day the word [*logos*—is this a quick allusion to the Prologue?] I have spoken will serve as judge, for I have not spoken on my own" (48b-49a).

Thus this cry is a final witness/appeal to the synagogue: Jesus' teaching is true, but since he does nothing on his own but speaks "just as the Father has told me" (v. 50), he is not a second god but a selfless window through which one looks to see the very reality of God the Father. So ends Book One.

HOMILETICAL REFLECTIONS

Both Gospel and epistle raise the question that is at the heart of Christianity: What is the reality of the divine, a reality that determines what is human reality? Is that underlying reality one of power defined as dominance and control over others, or is it that power which is self-giving love?

This may seem a banal, trivial question, but the answer we give determines the very world in which we live. If we live in a world in which God's power is defined as dominance and control, then the world is pictured to accord with that understanding. God will demand obedience, threaten sanctions for disobedience, and will be used for justification of human authorities who "model" themselves after that God. Human society will be based on authoritarian control by some over others. The individual will base his or her self-understanding on that understanding of power and will find self-worth to the extent that he or she rules or obeys according to the model set.

Early believers in Jesus had an alternative understanding of power and thus created a different world. They came to see that God's power was really the power of self-giving for others. Both Paul and John use the cross as the symbol of this new understanding of power. For both it is in the cross that the purest revelation of God shines—the glorification of the transcendent. God is not the God who demands and threatens; God is one who loves in a way extreme, even foolish, to human standards (i.e., the way of power in the ordinary world).

For both Paul and John this power is not to be identified as masochistic. It is not weakness masquerading as morality; it is not the reverse of what is true, a reversal necessitated because Christians are too weak to grasp after what belongs only to the strong. True, God's power does not look like the power that is successful in the ordinary world. But believers stake their lives on the faith that it is actually *that* power which is *real*, that power which is ultimately more powerful than that of dominance and control.

If this is God's use of power, then believers who want to live in the world of the Christ event must model their own corporate and individual lives accordingly. They must learn to practice the power of self-giving in their communities and in their individual self-understandings. Seeking to be faithful we reach for a world different from that of the ordinary, a new world in which God, communities, and selves relate to each other under the banner of self-giving love.

For believers who live, no doubt partially but with vision, in this new world, the ordinary, "false" world always threatens to drag them back into that old society. No one ever said it would be easy to maintain one's confidence in the new understanding of power. We all slip back and act out our relationships as if power were really domination and control. Paul and John at least show us a vision of what the new world can be like. And that is the ultimate value of the symbol of the cross.

No one ever said as well that it would be easy to convince others that this power is true power. Believers were a small minority in the days of Paul and John—and their way of contrasting the true and false shows that they had experienced often the refusal by others to listen sympathetically to the new understanding. We are in a minority today, and there are those who suspect that even many in the church do not really live out of the power of self-giving.

Perhaps we cannot convince by argument. Perhaps we are limited to manifesting in our communities what the alternative is, showing by our corporate lives the reality that stands over against the commonly accepted one. As someone has pointed out, in John mission has become witness. Maybe we are called today to witness the reality of the cross, not as a masochistic symbol of desired suffering, but as that which points to the ultimate power which is stronger than anything the false world can perceive.

Wednesday in Holy Week

FIRST LESSON: ISAIAH 50:4-9

(See the first lesson for the Sunday of the Passion.)

PSALMS 69 AND 70

Both of these psalms also belong to the category of the righteous, innocent sufferer. Psalm 69 is a long, somewhat rambling song by a person who is threatened by death, perhaps has been imprisoned, and who has enemies that threaten him, in part, presumably, because he is accused of stealing (v. 4). He has become shamed (vv. 7-8) and an outcast. Yet he says that it is zeal for the temple that has brought him to his low estate (v. 9, cited by John 2:17 to point to Jesus' death as having some relation to the temple event). The implication seems to be that the singer took an unpopular stand with regard to God and/or the temple (cf. also vv. 6-7, 9b-11).

The general complaint, that the psalmist has suffered unjustly in extreme ways, made it attractive to early Christians who were attempting to come to terms with the death of Jesus. The verse cited by the Gospels (v. 21) in the crucifixion account is part of the description of the enmity the psalmist's enemies have showered upon him. The reciter showers down threats upon the enemies in return (vv. 22-28), and the psalm ends with praise to God (vv. 30-36).

Psalm 70 is a brief song that is essentially identical with Psalm 40:13-17. In it the singer, under threat to his life, prays to God for deliverance from his enemies. He has perhaps also sought safety in the temple precincts.

SECOND LESSON: HEBREWS 9:24-28, 12:1-3; ROMANS 5:6-11

(For Hebrews 9:11-15 see the second lesson for Monday in Holy Week.)

Hebrews 9:24-28 is structurally very similar to 9:11-15. Both depict the movement of Christ, viewed in the one passage as sacrifice, in the other as High Priest, from earth to the heavenly sanctuary. In both the death of Christ is highlighted as "once for all," in distinction from the continual offerings of the earthly priests. The heavenly sanctuary functions as symbol of the perfection of the sacrifice, even at the cost of some straining of the analogy between earthly and heavenly (from what does the heavenly sanctuary need to be cleansed?—9:23).

The question again before us is how the analogy *functions* religiously. In 9:11-14 I suggested the weight lay in the phrase "purify our conscience from dead works" (v. 14). In 9:24-28 this idea is stated in other words by verse 26, "to remove sin by the sacrifice of himself." The word *removal* may have here a legal sense; the sacrifice is the ratification of a legal writ (note carefully that the material *between* our two passages has as its theme the new covenant). At any rate, so far 9:24-26 has said little that is new.

A remarkable advance in thought comes in verses 27-28. Verse 27 sets up the idea by listing common human fate. People live and die. After that comes judgment—an idea particularly indebted to Jewish apocalyptic, but perhaps known as well to certain forms of Greek thought. But of what does this judgment consist? Is this something to be feared? With what kind of confidence or dread does a person look forward to this fate?

Anxiety about this fate afflicts Christians as well as others. Hebrews, however, suggests that the Christ event should eliminate this anxiety just as the purification of conscience eliminates the correlate anxiety about guilt. Christ's second coming (the only place in the New Testament that identifies the eschatological appearance of Christ as the "second") will *not* be for judgment but for salvation *of those who are awaiting him*. Quite the contrary to Byzantine and medieval art, which portrays the resurrected Christ as the stern judge, Hebrews offers a Christ whose function is to remove impediments to relation to God, including the focus on the "second coming" as entirely for the salvation of believers.

What then is the appropriate stance of the believer, according to our author? She is one who *believes*, that is, is confident that the "once for all" event of Christ has erased guilt for her past sin and who can thus *anticipate eagerly* her ultimate fate as belonging to the saving Christ. The message of Hebrews is *assurance* for believers, the elimination of guilt of the past and dread before one's future. We may not reverberate easily with the constant metaphors of the sacrificial cult, but the purpose of the author is one that speaks across the barriers of the metaphor.

Hebrews 12:1-3, perhaps to our relief, for once leaves the metaphor of the sacrificial cult and takes another, drawn from the popular and well-known athletic events of its author's time. Chapter 11 has lifted up some of the great faith heroes of the past. In our passage they become spectators of the present contest. They are partisans urging on the contestants—the "we" of the church. "We" are exhorted to strip for the race and to run it with the necessary "perseverance." The contestants are not, however, to look in the stands for approbation (as happens, alas, in our own day) but to look ahead to the one who is running before us—the one who began and finished before us (the analogy may not be perfect here). At any rate, the Jesus who died and has been enthroned should be the athlete to be emulated.

That the race goes through, not around, the cross and shame doubtlessly speaks to the situation of the church addressed by the author. Elsewhere he exhorts them to be faithful even if that means persecution in its various forms (cf. 10:32-39; 13:13). The race is not all "fun and games." It is perhaps not accidental that this passage includes the only use of "cross" in the tract. (One could consult profitably Paul's occasional uses of the metaphor of the public arena—1 Cor. 4:9-13; 9:24-27.)

Romans 5:6-11. In chapter 5 of Romans Paul begins a long section that emphasizes the act of God in Christ as a completed event. This is captured in the opening sentence: "since we are justified by faith, we have peace with God through our Lord Jesus Christ" (5:1). 5:6-11 is a key passage that points to the meaning of that opening sentence. What does it mean to have peace with God and how is that related to being justified?

Verses 6-11 are carefully arranged. The backbone of the section is composed of three structurally similar clauses.

While we were—weak (v. 6)	Christ died—for ungodly
sinners (v. 8)	for us
enemies (v. 10)	reconciled us.

The result of this act seen in three ways climaxes in the theme of reconciliation and suggests that the clauses are arranged in ascending order of importance.

What is the human condition (Paul is certainly speaking universally here) of "being weak"? This question is not so easily answered. While Paul uses the adjective *weak* several times, there is really no adequate parallel in his letters to this statement in Romans. I take it that "weak" means essentially a condition where one is unable to do what one wishes, or what is needful. It is the condition of being powerless, that is, bound to a certain mode of being, unable to escape, to work one's way to a different place, or "world." Paul clearly thinks humans are living in a false world and are unable to do anything about it—they do not even know that they are in such a false world (cf. Rom. 1:18-23). To rectify this power-lessness—that is, to empower humans to become strong—Christ died.

The second characteristic of the human condition is sin. While this seems obvious, we need to be cautious before reading this sentence as we ordinarily do when we think about sin. Sin, for Paul, is not primarily specific acts of evil deeds (although it leads to those acts) but a condition of refusing to acknowledge who the real God is—a God of radical self-giving. God has been misinterpreted as a God who demands righteousness (for the Jew, righteousness according to Torah) and who threatens doom if this righteousness is not performed. Sin is then living in that false world in which God is falsely perceived and the self and society defined according to that tragically erroneous view of God. Christ died, says Paul, to show humans that they do live in a false world and to give people the possibility of leaving the false and entering the true world, based on a God perceived through the cross of Christ.

The third characteristic is hostility—and Paul says that it is hostility *toward God*. It is not God who is angry with humans (not "Sinners in the Hands of an Angry God"!), but it is humanity that is angry with God (cf. 2 Cor. 5:16-21)! This is one of the most remarkable insights of Paul, one that has so often been turned on its head in Christian theology. What does it mean?

It means, I think, that Paul has become aware, no doubt through his own personal struggles, that the "false" God engenders hostility and rebellion in humans because of the perceived demand of righteous performance. It is the same insight Luther had, engrossed in his own perceived sin while still a monk. He is reported to have said then, "I don't love God, I hate him!" Christ died to overcome this hostility by showing that this false God does not exist. God has been tragically misread. To read God truly out of the cross is to grasp that God is and has always been the caring, self-giving parent who grants life without any conditions.

Thus Paul sees the act of God in Christ as a powerful deed that overcomes the false perceptions that humanity has of God by revealing who God really is, freeing persons from the past and enabling them to see God and thus themselves and their world anew. The final word Paul speaks in this passage is to remind his hearers of the importance of reconciliation, because it is, I suspect, for Paul the final test of whether a person truly lives in faith. Faith has to mean acceptance of God as the giver; in such faith there need be no hostility.

GOSPEL: JOHN 13:21-35; MATTHEW 26:14-25

John 13:21-35. The events described in Book Two have already begun at 13:1. Here Jesus turns away from the world and addresses his disciples (the church) during the last evening of his life. This section will continue through chapter 17. This last evening begins, however, with one person present who belongs to the world outside, who is present at the footwashing and who thus presumably has his feet washed by Jesus. This inclusion may be traditional, since in the Synoptic tradition Judas is also present at the Last Supper.

Now comes our scene in which the betrayer is pointed to explicitly by Jesus (John has already referred to Judas in 13:2, 11, 18-19). It will conclude with Judas departing, so that the remainder of the discourse is with those who are truly called. (It is interesting that only John among the Gospels pictures the departure of Judas before the arrest scene.)

The story of Jesus' "prediction" of the betrayal is, of course, common to all the Gospels. John's version has its own distinctive features, however, and suggests that the basic story, known commonly in the early church, has been written so that specific Johannine interests are made clear.

In fact, it is perhaps not accurate to call John's version a prediction by Jesus—Jesus' role may be more active than that. John's picture of the passion is that Jesus (and God) is firmly in control. Jesus exercises power to lay down his life and take it up again (10:18). To Pilate he says that the governor has no power to take his life—it is given him from above (19:11). Thus it may be that John wants to say more than that Jesus simply knows in advance who will betray him.

There are indications that Jesus actually *causes* Judas's betrayal. Jesus deliberately gives Judas a bit of food (some have called this a magical portion), and it is only after this act that "Satan entered" into Judas. Jesus then commands Judas to act: "Do quickly what you are going to do." Judas obediently leaves, "and it was night." For John Jesus is in charge. The betrayal—of course a known item of tradition—is necessary for Jesus' death, and Jesus is as much in control over Judas as he is over Pilate.

This interpretation may be called into question by 13:2, but this verse should probably be translated, "The devil had already decided that Judas was to betray him." We must, of course, be careful of trying to find perfect agreement among the Gospel accounts, since many originally disparate items have been joined to make the final narratives.

In *verses 31-32*, the author ties together Judas's departure with glorification, just as he has already in chapter 12 linked the interest of the Greeks with the same glorification. The time of the crucifixion as the revelation of God's love draws ever closer, and with the betrayal now set, all the dynamic has been set in place. Jesus can now begin to address his true disciples (those who have been given him) and initiate them into the true meaning of discipleship. In the midst of darkness (v. 30) he discusses how they can live in the light.

Verses 33-35. Before Book Two the verb *agapan*, "to love" (John never uses the noun), occurs occasionally in various ways. In Book Two it becomes a dominant word and is used to describe the essential relationships among the participants—God, Jesus, and disciples. Only 1 John affirms that "God is love" (1 John 4:8), but it is clear that in the Gospel this word comes close to defining the essential characteristic of God's reality. The Gospel makes it equally clear that those who participate in God participate in that transcendent quality (e.g., 14:20-23).

In this passage, the first in which Jesus instructs the disciples, the emphasis is upon loving *one another* (e.g., love is reciprocal). Jesus' love for them is the model for their love for one another. And the content of this model? The text does not say here, but it will be clarified in 15:12-13, where it is Jesus' giving up of himself to death that is the exemplar for the disciples' loving.

The point in this passage, however, is not so much to define the precise meaning of loving as it is to point to the result of the disciples' loving one another: that is the manifestation that they are in relation to Jesus—they are indeed his disciples. This is the same hard claim that the Gospel makes elsewhere in other words, that the purpose of the church is to manifest the reality of God to the world. Just as the self-giving loving of Jesus manifests God's glory, so the loving-one-another in the church is that, and that only, which is the continuing manifestation of the reality of God.

In the interests of following the main dynamic of the plot of this material, I have leaped over one conundrum dear to the minds of many. Our passage contains the first occurrence in the Gospel of that enigmatic disciple identified in the text as "the one whom Jesus loved." Who is this "beloved disciple?" The simple answer is that no one knows, despite the numerous proposals that have been made. Whoever he is, in this story he is not crucial to the plot movement, and it is wise not to get sidetracked.

Matthew 26:14-25. This section of the passion narrative also focuses on the theme of Judas's betrayal. In fact, Matthew has more interest than even John in the problems raised by this tradition (cf. 27:3-10). That one of Jesus' intimates in some way betrayed him to Jewish authorities seems to be one of the bedrock pieces of fact. This fact could not be ignored, perhaps because it provided fuel for Jewish maligning of the Jesus communities. Matthew seems especially sensitive to such maligning (cf., e.g., the way he treats the "stealing of the body motif" and perhaps the illegitimate birth of Jesus). Matthew deals with each of these attacks by providing counterlegends, defending a faith interpretation of the "events" over against hostile interpretation.

John, as seen above, handles the difficulty by having Jesus himself provoke the betrayal. Matthew is content to follow Mark in having Jesus know in advance that the betrayal is to take place. In fact, he heightens this by adding verse 25 to the Markan original. One could read Mark 14:17-21 in such a way that Jesus knows that *someone* is to betray him but he does not know *who*—at least the name of Judas is not mentioned. The *reader* of Mark knows, of course, because the initiating story of the agreement between Judas and the authorities has already been told (14:10-11). With the addition of Matthew 26:25, the author makes it clear that Jesus *did* know who the betrayer was.

Verses 14-16.   Matthew narrates Mark's account but adds the detail of the "thirty pieces of silver." This introduces the rationale of greed as the cause of Judas's deed and prepares the way for the elaborate (if confusing) story of the aftermath of this agreement (27:3-10). The whole sequence functions in the Matthean narrative to explain away, as best as possible, the heinous crime of betrayal by an intimate.

Verses 17-19.   Matthew shortens Mark's account, removing the miraculous elements from it. Here it serves simply as a necessary prelude to the supper itself. The long and inconclusive debate about whether Jesus' last meal was actually a Passover meal cannot be entered here. It is noteworthy, however, that both in Mark and in Matthew this pericope (which may have been one of the latest additions in Mark to the narrative) is the only one in which it is explicitly said that the meal is a Passover.

Matthew adds the ominous sentence, "My time [*kairos*] is near." Clearly this points forward to the decisive "time" of the death (even though the term *kairos* is not a key theological term for him).

Verses 20-25.   In the early church the issue of table fellowship was important—who could legitimately sit at table with another? Galatians 2:11-14 illustrates how divisive such an issue could become. But this sensitivity is itself a reflection of the importance attached to table fellowship in the ancient world. To sit at table with another was to express mutual respect and mutual responsibility. Table fellowship depended upon a code of honor, in which it was assumed that each respected the other. To betray someone who dipped into the same bowl at table was an extraordinarily despicable act.

I emphasize this because we have all become so domesticated to the sacred story that it no longer offends as it should, and as it would have offended the early hearers. It is, indeed, but one of several such despicable acts that dot the passion stories. There is no relief from the horror, unless it is, perhaps, the pericope of the Eucharist itself, and even that is focused on the imminent death.

Matthew follows Mark's narrative closely. He adds, however, a specific question by Judas. The disciples' and Judas's questions all imply a negative answer. The questions are different only in the address to Jesus. The disciples call Jesus "Lord"; Judas calls him "rabbi" (or "my master"). In the Markan account, the disciples' question has no titular address. Thus Matthew has "borrowed" the titles from elsewhere. The title *kyrios* is common to his narrative and it is natural that he adds it here. The title *rabbi* he gets from Judas's address to Jesus in Gethsemane (26:49—as in Mark). Some scholars see in this difference Judas's lesser deference to Jesus; since the titles mean the same thing (or can), however, it is precarious to lean on this difference for too much homiletical value.

What is important is the fact that Matthew introduces the specific question by Judas, to which Jesus makes a simple response, "you say." These words can have a number of nuances, but scholars seem agreed that, at least in this context, it implies a subtle but positive answer. Something like, "Your own words bring the guilt upon yourself, by speaking truly." This very response by Jesus occurs twice more in the passion narrative: once after the High Priest's question, "Tell us if you are the Christ, the Son of God" (26:63f.); the second time, after Pilate's question, "Are you the king of the Jews?" (27:11). The response is given to enemies, is expressed without any bombast, but nevertheless implies that the enemy has spoken truly (as enemies sometimes do).

HOMILETICAL REFLECTIONS

Everybody dies; so what is so special about the death of Jesus? (So the curious ask over and over.)

Believer: But it was the death of the Son of God!

Curious: I don't believe that he was so special.

B: But he died such a horrible death!

C: Come on. How many people have died such deaths, some more horrible than Jesus'? The Romans must have crucified thousands—so what is different about this one crucifixion?

B: *But he was betrayed and abandoned, and he died all alone!*

C: OK. That doesn't make Jesus' death unique, but it does make it tough.

But he was betrayed and abandoned, and he died all alone. We believers have become so inured by the retelling of the story that we do not really know, probably, where it begins to hook us. Hook us it does, but why? Today's Gospel readings give us some clue, I think, about one dimension of the story that is so horrifying. Yes, Jesus died a violent death; yes, he was innocent of the charges made; yes, he died young. But he also died betrayed and abandoned, and he died all alone.

By its very definition, betrayal makes no sense—and in this sense-lessness lies its horror. A betrayer does not refer to someone who has always been opposed to the person. A betrayer means one who once was an ally, one who supported the cause or the person involved. A betrayer does not even mean simply a person who changes his mind—who might come to me and say, "Let's talk this through. I think I've changed my mind and will thus have to leave you."

A betrayer means someone who has been an ally and who suddenly (or so it seems) turns publicly against a cause. A betrayer is a *friend* who suddenly makes a violent act expressing rejection and hostility toward that which he once espoused.

Thus to the betrayed it makes no sense. It is the seeming meaninglessness that gives betrayal its specific horror. But I was always her friend! I gave him the best years of my life! Why didn't she come and talk it through with me? How could he desert the group just at this crucial time? Why did he pull the rug out from under us, when he had been our ally? I can understand why she changed her mind, but did she have to make it public in such a hostile way?

There is probably no one with any life experience who hasn't felt this horror of betrayal at one time or another. And it is, I suggest, its apparent senselessness that makes us beat our heads against the wall. There are doubtlessly reasons for every betrayal, and we seek to make sense of the act by rationalizing it as best we can. But in the final analysis, it remains an absurdity.

The New Testament texts are no different. Judas's betrayal obviously was horrifying to the early church, and it attempted to explain it as best it could. Judas was a bad character anyway. He was a thief; he was greedy for money; Jesus really made it happen. Hardly anybody reads these attempts today thinking that they reveal the heart of Judas. That heart remains inaccessible to us, as well as to the early believers. In other words, from our perspective the deed was and remains meaningless.

In fact, the entire passion narrative is in this sense meaningless. Whatever theological interpretation one wishes to place upon the person of Jesus, the historical data, as sparse as it is, portrays him as one who was committed to a God who cared for others. He does not appear violent or revolutionary. There seems to be no observable rational reason why it was "right" to put Jesus to death, why his disciples were so spineless, why Judas betrayed him.

Thus (or so it seems to me) one of the profound questions raised by the passion narrative, exampled here by the betrayal of Judas, is how to live one's life in the face of apparent meaninglessness. Our temptation is either to rationalize what is going on or to avoid it by fleeing into some form of fantasy.

Is there some other way? At its best the passion narrative confronts the meaninglessness of the events with Jesus' steadfast faith in God. Here meaninglessness is not denied or avoided (although John does go in that direction). What gives Jesus the power to name the meaninglessness for what it is is his stubborn faith in God and God's claim upon him. It is saying, "This makes no sense to me, but my primary commitment is to live a certain way before the God in which I believe, and this I will do no matter how senseless life seems."

One way to view this is to return to Paul's vision of the true and the false worlds. They are radically different worlds because they have such different gods. One world makes no sense to the other. Just as the authorities could not understand Jesus—he probably made no sense to them—so the early believers could make no sense out of the events of the passion. To say that Jesus stubbornly maintained his faith in God in the face of meaninglessness is to say that Jesus remained true to his vision of the true world, in the face of the apparent power of the false world to act out its ritual of domination. Just so, believers are not called to understand life; they are called to a faithfulness that sustains them in the midst of a world that makes no sense.

Maundy Thursday/Holy Thursday

Lectionary	First Lesson	Psalm	Second Lesson	Gospel
Episcopal	Exod. 12:1-14a	Ps. 78:14-20, 23-25	I Cor. 11:23-26	John 13:1-15 or Luke 22:14-30
Roman Catholic	Exod. 12:1-8, 11-14	Ps. 116b:12-13, 15-16, 17-18	I Cor. 11:23-26	John 13:1-15
Revised Common	Exod. 12:1-4, (5-10), 11-15	Ps. 116:1-2, 12-19	I Cor. 11:23-26	John 13:1-17, 31b-35
Lutheran	Exod. 12:1-14	Ps. 116:10-17	I Cor. 11:17-32 or 11:23-26	John 13:1-17, 34

FIRST LESSON: EXODUS 12:1-15

The selection of this narrative grounding the Passover celebration in a crucial moment at the beginning of the exodus is, of course, due to the understanding that Jesus' last meal was a Passover meal. Whether this was actually so may be doubted, but ever since the Gospel stories reached their final form, Christians have read their passion story in tandem with the Passover story of Israel. There is actually an interesting parallel here: At some point Israel inserted its sacred festival of Passover into a historical context; just so, early Christians inserted Jesus' last meal into the Passover context.

What was in Israel originally an agricultural festival (actually very likely already a joining together of two such festivals—Passover and unleavened bread) has been grafted into the narrative of the release from bondage. Thereafter what Passover *means* is inexorably associated with that narrative. Once the last meal of Jesus and his disciples is grafted into the Passover festival, what the Last Supper *means* for Christians is equally tied to what that festival had come to mean for the Judaism of the first century.

Exodus 12 states the connection of the agricultural festival with the historical event more clearly than any of the other references in Scripture (cf. Num. 9:1-14; Josh. 5:10-12; 2 Kings 23:21-23; 2 Chron. 30:1-27; 35:1-19; Ezra 6:19-22). According to most scholars Exodus 12:1-20 is a late (finally Priestly) account, which should reflect how the Passover was interpreted during the second temple period. Verses 1-13 describe Passover; verses 14-20, the feast of unleavened bread.

This late version gives instructions for and commemorates the final night before the Israelites are allowed to depart from Egypt. Since the story reflects liturgical practice, it functions both as the past (what happened) and the present (what is to happen regularly in ritual). The two are linked together because the ritual remembers and reenacts the past (cf. 12:14b,

24-27). God is ready to strike dead all the firstborn of people and animals in Egypt. Each Israelite family is to sacrifice a lamb and put some of its blood on the doorposts of its house. That will be a sign to God to "pass over" that house so that its firstborn will not be killed.

Moreover, the eating of the sacrificial meal is to symbolize the intense preparation for departure. The meal is to be eaten "on the run" as it were, in complete readiness for the move. One is even, presumably, to eat the food with one hand while one's staff is in the other (v. 11).

Thus the Passover sacrificial meal reminds its participants that they are part of that congregation liberated from bondage by God's extraordinary and tenacious power. It recalls for them their ancestors' willingness to march into the wilderness, with little assurance of the outcome. According to the account in our text, "eating on the run" is a crucial part of one's memory that is to be translated into one's present attitude toward the outside world. One can live by the "fleshpots of Egypt," or one can dare the scary move into an unknown future. One must balance security over against sitting loose to what is present so that one may be open to God's call.

In the second temple period the Passover festival was a pilgrim festival. That meant it could not be celebrated except in Jerusalem. Many people from outside Jerusalem, even from the Diaspora, traveled to be there for that time. Josephus gives us ample evidence of the overcrowded scene during these pilgrim festivals. One could well imagine that the pure religious expression of the festival described in Exodus 12 was diluted or broadened (according to your perspective) by all the attendant dimensions of such "holiday" occasions. It was a time of relief from home, of enjoyment in the "big city," of seeing the sights, of the celebrative time of the meal itself.

The more somber elements of the symbolism may have been lost on all except the pious. For any early Christians, who were aware of the complex dimensions of what actually happened in Jerusalem at such times, the story of a small circle gathered to celebrate the Passover with death impending for its leader must have been heard by believers with a particular poignancy.

PSALM 116

Psalm 116 is a personal thanksgiving for God's deliverance from the threat of death. It follows the typical pattern of protestation of faithfulness in God despite the dangers that the reciter thinks surround him. What these dangers are is not clear. It may be personal attacks by others (v. 11) or bondage (v. 16). Verse 15 seems to mean that God cares too much for the faithful (in whose number the psalmist includes himself) to allow them to suffer death.

The scene of the psalm is a public act in the temple, where the psalmist, on the one hand, offers praise to God for deliverance and, on the other, offers vows and thanksgiving offerings (vv. 13—where the "cup of salvation" may be a libation—14, 17-18).

SECOND LESSON: I CORINTHIANS 11:17-32

The focus in today's epistle is Paul's recital of the liturgical act of the "Lord's Supper." Yet Paul mentions this only because he has something to say to the Corinthians about the *context* in which they observe that act. To hear Paul fairly and, indeed, to understand what *he* thinks the act itself means, we have to pay attention to Paul's blistering attack against what he hears is going on in the church assembly. Not everything is clear, but we can reconstruct a general picture.

In verse 17 Paul continues his comments about the meetings of the community (he has begun this at 11:2). He uses terminology that he introduced in chapter 1 about divisions and ruptures in the life of the church. There he associated the divisions with baptism; here he relates them to the Lord's Supper. The liturgical life of the church may not be the only place where these divisions are manifest, but it is remarkable that he explicitly associates them directly with worship (cf. also chaps. 12–14). What a far cry from our own day, when the liturgical events cover over splits in the fabric of the church!

Indeed, Paul even claims that "when you come together, it is not really to eat the Lord's supper" (v. 20). Does he mean that they have no interest in the liturgical act (i.e., intentionality), or does he mean that, while they intend to, their actions are of such foreign spirit that they do not *really* participate? Perhaps both.

In the Greek world, associations of various sorts (e.g., burial groups, workers' guilds) were popular. At the meetings meals were important and sometimes were festive occasions. Food and drink were enjoyed and portions were often meted out according to levels of importance within the group (i.e., the leaders got larger ones than the others). In the Corinthian church, members may have been bringing to the common meal, which had as part of its ceremony the Lord's Supper, some of the same expectations they had known from other associations (and in which they perhaps still participated).

They had come together for a good time! They brought their own food and drink and, perhaps, sat in coteries separated from the others (could this be why Paul complains about divisions?). Paul thinks this is inappropriate for two reasons. One is that the importance of the Lord's Supper itself is diminished. The other is that these divisions separate some from

others and "humiliate those who have nothing" (v. 22). What Paul seems
to picture is several groups of friends (perhaps reflecting economic status)
isolating themselves from others, not paying attention to the community
as *the* group and ignoring the ostensible purpose for which the group has
assembled. Does that sound familiar?

Paul then repeats the central liturgical act *in order to* call the groups to
the real center of the purpose of the meeting. Rightly understood, he thinks,
the liturgy, far from glossing over the differences and leaving them un-
touched, should eliminate the differences. It has the power to overcome
distractions and deviations and reunite all in a common purpose that tran-
scends the fun and games. To know truly what is going on at the Lord's
Supper is to create a true "coming together."

What then is this center and what does it mean for Paul? What Paul
cites is so basically close to the description in Mark 14:22-25 that it is
obvious we have before us the actual liturgy practiced in many early
churches. While scholars like to focus on the differences between the
Markan and Pauline accounts, one must begin with the similarities and
leave most of the fine differences to the commentators.

The event is simplicity itself: Two words, one about body, the other
about blood, both related to the death of Jesus. Mark says that the act is
a covenant sacrifice—perhaps understood as a covenant renewal ceremony.
In the Greek churches reflected in the Pauline account, the covenant has
become the *new* covenant. The Lord's Supper is no longer just a renewal
of God's relationship with Israel; it is *new*, almost certainly because the
covenant now includes Gentiles as members of God's people. The death
of Jesus is thus portrayed as a *covenant* sacrifice (i.e., one that ratifies a
mutual agreement), not a sacrifice that deals with sin. Even the phrase
about the body "for you" in no way points explicitly to an expiation for
sin. The death of Jesus creates a new covenant and thus a new fellowship.

Also crucial is the command associated with each part: "Do this in
remembrance of me." The meal looks primarily to the past. It is in part a
meal of remembrance of the deeds of the founder of the cult. This is,
perhaps, an assimilation to the kinds of honoring of gods and cult leaders
in the Greek world. Paul has no problem with the meal as a remembrance
meal, because it enables him to focus on death, rather than resurrection.

This focus comes out clearly in verse 26, which may have been part of
the words at the meal or may be Paul's present comment on the meaning
of the liturgy. Here the point of the liturgical acts is summarized: "You
proclaim the Lord's death." There is no mention of the resurrection (either
of Jesus or of the believers) and the one reference to the future, "until he
comes," is taut and ambiguous. What will happen "when he comes"? The
liturgical act does not seem to deal with that.

Having laid out the drama that Paul thinks ought to overcome the problems, he turns to address responsible preparation for the event. People need to know what they are doing! Not to know, Paul thinks, in his surprisingly crude connection between faith and physiology, brings not only judgment but also physical illnesses and death. Not to know what one is doing in this central liturgical act has serious consequences.

The key question remains: How does Paul think awareness of what is going on in the liturgy can serve to overcome the divisions in the community that have led to contempt and humiliation of some of the members? He does not explicitly say, and attempts to answer the question must be made cautiously.

Two points seem worthy of consideration: (1) The act is about a new covenant sealed by the death of the Lord—and a new covenant means a new people called together. This is the basis for "coming *together*," not for a segmenting into interest groups. The divisions thus belie the very meaning of the event that ostensibly brings them together. This must be what Paul means when he says they do not come together to eat the Lord's Supper.

(2) The new community brought into being by the death of the Lord by definition allows for no valuations of people that lead some to be, or consider themselves, "better" than others. All have been equally gifted by that death; thus all are equal in the new covenant fellowship. Divisions imply such valuations and therefore mean that the true reality of the gift of the death has not been perceived. Elsewhere Paul speaks of this by his slogan, "justification by grace." In Christ all are equal, because all have been equally gifted. When the fellowship of the new covenant comes together, each member must be honored as an equal sharer in the covenant.

GOSPEL: JOHN 13:1-17

Chapter 13 begins Book Two of the Gospel; Jesus turns away from the world to those who are his intimates. On the last night he speaks at length to "his own" and through them to the church of the author's day. But before the lengthy discourses begin (in chap. 14), two events are described. One is the initiating scene—the washing of the disciples' feet; the other, the sending out of Judas to betray (cf. the second lesson for Wednesday of Holy Week). The footwashing is a startling event—a leader acting out a parable of service.

Verse 1 can best be seen as an introduction to the entire Book Two (chaps. 13–17, or 13–20). It locates the timing of the scene (note well that it is different from that of the Synoptics, since it is *not* the first night of Passover) and its significance: It is the hour, the decisive moment, of

Jesus' departure—his death, resurrection, and exaltation. This verse also introduces the theme of loving "his own" that are in the world. The contrast is briefly but clearly stated: Jesus departs the world; "his own" remain in it. This threat of separation and loss will be discussed in detail in the chapters to come.

"He loved them to the end." The Greek behind "to the end" can just as easily be translated "completely." The author has a penchant for double meanings, and it is perhaps likely that he is aware of both meanings and finds each one suitable. Jesus loves them completely, and he loves them to the very end—to his death. Ultimately there is no distinction. Were he not to love them by accepting his death, he would not be loving them completely.

The footwashing event itself can be divided into two distinct sections, each of them providing a different, if complementary, interpretation of the scene. Verses 12-20 think of the act of Jesus as an act of service; it is an example to be emulated by the disciples. The first section (vv. 2-11), which includes the actual description of the act, implies that the washing is connected somehow with Jesus' salvatory coming, is unique, and thus nonexemplary. Most scholars posit separate traditions to explain the differences in meaning. Both, however, are in the text before us and it seems wise to deal with each interpretation as of equal value and even to raise the question of what relationship there might be between the two.

Interwoven into the composite story is the thread of Judas' betrayal (vv. 2, 11, 18-19.). The act of Jesus' service takes place in the presence of and, in some sense, *for* the betrayer as well as for others.

Verses 2-11. The participants at the supper are assumed to be reclining on couches, with their feet extending outward, away from the table (cf. the story of the anointing: the Gospel for Monday of Holy Week). Jesus suddenly and without precedent rises from his couch, removes his outer garment (or strips naked—the text can mean either), ties a towel around him, pours water into a bowl and without comment washes the feet of his disciples. What does such action mean? It *should* mean a servile act for a superior by an inferior. Clearly some explanation is necessary here!

In Book Two the author uses dialogue to lead the reader through his argument (cf., e.g., chap. 14). The comments of the disciples serve, somewhat similarly to those in the Dialogues of Plato, to provide Jesus the opportunity to make his pronouncements. Here Peter is the foil. He protests Jesus' action: It is too humiliating for a master to perform! Jesus cryptically (v. 7) does not really clarify the situation; he simply adds this action to the list of those the disciples will not understand until "later" (cf. 2:22; 12:16). That is, in some unexplained way the footwashing is tied to a future explanation. The *reader* (who is inevitably more omniscient than the disciples at this moment in the plot) would assume that that explanation will come with understanding of death/resurrection.

Peter then makes explicit his protest. He is too good a disciple to allow his master to be humiliated before him (v. 8). In the same way Peter will claim to be a good disciple in following Jesus to death (13:37). Jesus responds with a statement, the meaning of which is hardly transparent: "Unless I wash you, you have no share with me." It means at least that Jesus' act of washing is essential to belonging to him and sharing in the salvation he makes present. How this is to be understood can only be inferred. Is it meant literally or figuratively? Then Peter, still uncomprehending, responds with a request that apparently asks for more (a quantitative understanding of salvation?). In the dialogue it functions as a setup for Jesus' response.

"One who has bathed does not need to wash [except for the feet] but is entirely clean" (v. 10). The word here translated "bathe" is different from the word translated elsewhere in this story as "wash," and is occasionally used in early Christianity to refer to baptism. The words in brackets are omitted by only a few textual witnesses, but there are a number of scholars who think the shorter reading is original. The shorter reading *does* make better sense of an obscure statement. This statement by Jesus is the concluding one of this section (except for v. 10b, which returns to the theme of Judas). It therefore must be climactic, but what can it mean?

Jesus has implied (v. 7) that the footwashing is tied to the death/resurrection. He has said (v. 8) that it is essential if one is to have a share in the reality Jesus brings. He now says (v. 10) that the footwashing is complete in itself and needs no expansion, such as (for example) further washing rituals. According to some scholars this verse points to the sufficiency of the footwashing as a *symbol* of the death of Jesus. The complete sufficiency of the footwashing really says no more than that the death is completely sufficient for salvation. In that case the footwashing as *event* (once for all or repeated in ritual) is unimportant.

But what if the footwashing was a ritual action performed regularly in the Johannine church? In that case the event retains significance, although it may still function symbolically (in the same way that the Lord's Supper does). Some scholars actually see in the word *bathe* an allusion to the baptism, as if this event functions in the same way as a baptismal event (or perhaps even refers to baptism).

Our inability to be certain about the precise meaning of the dialogue doubtlessly stems from ignorance about the details of the Johannine church and its practices. At least this much is clear: The footwashing refers to

Jesus' sufficient salvatory act, an act that will be most clearly visible in the self-giving death.

Verses 11-17. The footwashing, interpreted in verses 6-10 as a salvatory act (at least pointing to such act), is here an act of service and self-giving. Jesus, though lord and teacher, has performed an act of service for his followers. This is an example to be imitated, a model for actions his followers are to do to "one another."

Verse 16 repeats a common observation which has been picked up by Q (Matt. 10:24; Luke 6:40), and will be repeated by John in 15:20, there to refer to persecution. Verse 17, however, expresses a remarkable judgment. Only here in the Gospel does Jesus express a *makarismos*, a statement of "blessing," upon anyone (the only other occurrence in John of the formula is 20:29).

What does a *makarismos* say and why is it placed here? The phrase should best be translated "Happy are you if [when] you do these things." It is approbation of a *present* state or possible present state of a person. It is being in the right place at the right time, doing the right thing! That is, the expression does not primarily point to some future reward for present service; it affirms, rather, that the present service is a state of happiness, or "rightness." The antecedent of "these things" is ambiguous, but in this context the author must want to refer to the service of footwashing. Perhaps he is thinking of all kinds of serving one another. To serve others is to be in a happy (blessed) state (which is not the same thing as to be in a state of happiness!).

What is the relationship between these two interpretations given to the act of footwashing? Do they hang in the air as independent, unrelated meanings, or is there an inner connection?

I believe there is an inner connection, one that is based in the heart of John's theology. Jesus is the revelation of the reality of God (God's glory). For humans "salvation" means seeing that glory and *participating* in it. "Seeing is believing," and believing is participation in that glory. But what happens when Jesus departs, when the light, the glory, leaves the world? Jesus' answer in the farewell discourses is that the Holy Spirit (the Paraclete) will take his place. But the Paraclete must have a "flesh," just as the Logos had in Jesus. This new "flesh" is the church; the Paraclete through the church replicates the saving act of the Logos.

Thus as Jesus serves, as he loves, as he lays down his life, as he washes feet, so the disciples are to live, to witness to the very light that shone in the Logos. As the light in Jesus is revelatory of the reality of God, so the service of and in the church replicates that salvatory light. Jesus serves and reveals God in the act of footwashing. And the disciples, modeling their service after Jesus, also participate in the reality of God and reveal God's glory. This is why they are "happy" in that replication, because they are then living in eternal life when they reveal God's glory through their self-giving.

(For comment on 13:31-35, see the Gospel for Wednesday in Holy Week.)

HOMILETICAL REFLECTIONS

The cumulative effect of these readings—especially if one adds those previously dealt with in this volume—is one of unrelieved emphasis upon the somber, some would say the lugubrious. In the world around us, the taste of our culture dictates an avoidance of such somberness. We want more sitcoms! Lugubriousness and masochism are out of fashion. Sacrificial service may be OK for some (let's read about it in the *Reader's Digest!*), but we have no time for such extravagancies.

Even those of us within the tradition who appreciate that it is only proper at this season of the liturgical year to hear such passages read and sermons preached on them may get a bit edgy at the unrelieved tension. Enough is enough! When will Easter come? Maybe the cultured despisers are right in saying this season only proves Nietzsche right—Christians love to wallow in the exaltation of suffering.

The irony in this is that there is no lack of suffering in the "real world." In fact, because of worldwide communications we today know about more suffering than any previous culture. Horrendous situations parade by us through the news media with such lightning speed that we can hardly learn the names of places and groups before the next calamity strikes. Nor is all the suffering "somewhere else." We know more about what is happening to our neighbors, and we have more technical terms (and concomitant self-help groups) to describe our problems than any previous culture. The proclamation of the moral degeneration of our society is so touted by preachers of whatever persuasion that hardly anyone listens anymore—but what they claim is probably true.

What we celebrate in one season of the year pales in comparison with what is read in the newspapers and seen on TV every day. And yet we are smiled at because we take the suffering of one man too seriously! How can we explain this?

Clearly we have failed to communicate to others the connection that exists between the story of Jesus and the suffering of our world. But have we made that connection for ourselves? If we isolate Jesus' suffering as a single, unique story of God's Son, then we do not help ourselves or our world see the connection.

What if we learned how these events of the past that we celebrate this week *could interpret our own present world and its suffering*? Could they give us a *paradigm* that helps us better to grasp what is going on? And can they give us a way to respond to the incredibly massive suffering of the world in some way other than to run from it in horror?

I think that the paradigm presented by the passion story is about self-giving. For believers self-giving is a life made possible by the grace of God that secures their own existence. Such self-giving is human reality. It is "authentic humanity," not something added on as a work of super-erogation. The authentic person lives out of strength (cf. the second lesson for Tuesday of Holy Week) and discovers in this life true meaning: "Happy is the one who does these things."

But there is another side to the paradigm. A person free to give herself runs into conflict with a society driven by anxiety toward expressions of aggression and domination. The world lives out of arrogance and brutality and runs roughshod over whatever self-giving it encounters, often without ever noticing it. When the world does see it, it mocks the self-giving person as ridiculous and trivial.

The passion story *can* serve as a paradigm for what goes on in our world. It describes the apparent failure of self-giving to be "successful" and suggests why it is that arrogance and the desperate need for self-assertion always seem to win. It shows that desperate arrogance seems to delight in causing rather than easing pain. The paradigm also, however, puts us in our obedient place in the face of domination. It calls us to realize our authentic humanity even if it leads to rejection, isolation, and pain.

Yes, the world smiles at our attention to the suffering of one man. If it only knew what the deep meaning of this story is, it would rage and gnash its teeth! To communicate to that world the depths we see in Jesus' passion would not make it more sympathetic to the story; it would rather shake the foundations! What is paradigm to Christianity is antiparadigm to the world.

Is this, then, what Christian faith means? Faith is the commitment to self-giving as actualization of our humanity, a faith that is awakened and strengthened in the story of Jesus' death. And strong faith is the commitment to self-giving in the face of the world's rejection of it as folly and weakness. Telling the story of Jesus thus gives us a paradigm for interpreting that world and for the new brought into existence by the Christ event. The paradigm gives us strength to participate in an alternate reality in which self-giving, even if it leads to suffering, is that which enables us to be truly human as God has created us to be. "Happy are you if you do these things!"

Good Friday

Lectionary	First Lesson	Psalm	Second Lesson	Gospel
Episcopal	Isa 52:13—53:12 or Gen. 22:1-18 or Wis. 2:1, 12-24	Ps. 22:1-21	Heb. 10:1-25	John (18:1-40) 19:1-37
Roman Catholic	Isa. 52:13—53:12	Ps. 31:2, 6, 12-13, 15-17, 25	Heb.4:14-16; 5:7-9	John 18:1-19, 42
Revised Common	Isa. 52:13—53:12	Psalm 22	Heb. 10:16-25 or 4:14-16; 5:7-9	John 18:1—19:42
Lutheran	Isa. 52:13—53:12 or Hosea 6:1-6	Ps.22:1-23	Heb. 4:14-16; 5:7-9	John 18:1—19:42 or 19:17-30

FIRST LESSON: ISAIAH 52:13—53:12

This passage, so deeply baptized into the Christian understanding of Jesus, and so "memorized" as the most important pointer in the Old Testament to the suffering of Jesus, is difficult to analyze dispassionately. The image of a despised and suffering "savior" figure is so vividly described that the passage affects deeply people of all persuasions. Since we do not know who this servant was or was to be, people inevitably see the identity of the servant differently. For Christians it somehow points toward Jesus in his suffering; for Jews it seems an appropriate symbol for the history of Israel, as it has suffered from the hands of others through the centuries.

This much, however, needs to be said at the beginning. The song is an assessment of the *meaning* of a person's life and death (whether the person is historical or symbolic). Just so, the passion stories in the Gospels are assessments of the meaning of Jesus' life and death. There is no question but that the two assessments, so widely separated in time, are closely similar in content. Such a life and death are claimed to be effective in healing the lives of others. We all struggle with the provocation this claim causes in our self-serving attempts to create a safe world for ourselves. Thus the fourth servant song will always be an ally with other instances of such challenges to our safety, whether that instance be the story of Jesus, the story of Israel, or modern figures such as Gandhi or Martin Luther King, Jr.

The song is, most simply seen, divided into three sections. The *first* section, 52:13-15, is a speech by God proclaiming the ultimate "fate" of the servant—that is, it looks ahead, beyond the narration of the second section. The *second* section, 53:1-10 (or 11ab), is a statement by a "we," describing the past and assigning meaning to that past. Section *three*, verses 11 (or 11cd)-12, is a return to the speech of God, again a proclamation of the ultimate result of the act of the servant and a promise of reward.

Section 1: 52:13-15. Verse 13 pronounces at the beginning the "success" of the servant. He accomplishes what God intended of him; thus he will be honored. This section clearly has a political context. The servant will be exalted (as an enthroned king?); he will have political effect upon national groups. This effect is caused by a "new knowledge" that, presumably, the servant brings either through his teaching or, more likely, through the meaning assessed his life, as will be described in section 2. Is this language "real" in that it speaks of an effect that actually took place? Or is it the usual political hyperbole so commonly ascribed to kings in the Ancient Near East, and reflected in the political rhetoric of the Old Testament (e.g., Psalm 2)?

Section 2: 53:1—53:10 (11ab). These verses describe the fate of the servant and assess meaning upon that fate from the standpoint of a "we." Who is this "we"? Is it the kings and nations mentioned in the preceding section? Is it Israel? Is it a group of people within Israel? Is it a prophet speaking for Israel or a group within? All these possibilities have been suggested by interpreters. In my judgment it is wisest to take the most modest or minimalist approach and to suggest that the "we" denotes a group within Israel which has come to understand the meaning of the death as effective, while it may be that none or few others, either in or outside Israel, agreed with that interpretation.

What is the meaning "they" see in the servant? The "outside" story seems to be something like this: He was unimpressive, even despicable in appearance. His mission was not taken seriously. He was attacked but he did not resist (did not rebel?); he was executed (v. 8) and buried (v. 9). On the *outside* his life and mission was a failure. There is indication that at the time of the events even the "we" did not see any positive meaning in them (vv. 2:b, 3d, 4b).

But the "we" now see those events differently. For them, the servant was truly the messenger of God (v. 1). He was unjustly persecuted for his message (8a). It was actually "we" who were the sinners (vv. 5-6, 8d). In this sense "he was wounded for our transgressions." Somehow the servant was the scapegoat for the true guiltiness of the larger group. So far, while the language of the song is moving, there is nothing truly novel about such an assessment. Leaders often die "for" their followers—that is, the leaders are punished while the followers are not.

The assessment, however, goes beyond this. This life/death is effective for healing others: "Upon him was the punishment that made us whole, and by his bruises we are healed" (v. 5b). What can this mean? Does it mean that something in the political situation was changed because of that death? Does it mean that something happened internally in Israel, as a result of the shock and subsequent reflection upon his death? It is impossible to know.

So far, I have avoided referring to the "resurrection" of the servant. Does the song say he was brought back to life after his death? This is hard to imagine; our earliest specific reference in the Old Testament to a resurrection of the dead does not occur until the book of Daniel, written some 250 years later. More likely the thought is that as others, after his death, become aware of his significance, his following will increase and in this sense he will "see his offspring."

Section 3: verses 11 (11cd)-12. Key here is the startling statement: "The righteous one, my servant, shall make many righteous." "To make righteous" is a legal term and refers to the act of the judge in declaring innocent (whatever the actual state is) and restoring the accused to the life of the community. The phrase is in parallel with "and he shall bear their iniquities" and suggests confidence that the death of the servant will somehow restore "all we who have gone astray" to true knowledge of and fellowship with God.

PSALMS 22 AND 31

(See the Psalms for Passion Sunday.)

SECOND LESSON: HEBREWS 4:14-16; 5:7-9; 10:16-25

The first two readings focus on Jesus' human situation of suffering; the third, on the new covenant.

Hebrews 4:14-16. Verse 14 reiterates the lordly, saving activity of Jesus' exaltation as God's Son and exhorts the hearers to "hold fast to [their] confession." That he urges them to do so suggests, as is said elsewhere in the sermon, that some believers are, or are in danger of, falling away from that confession.

Verses 15 and 16 then give one practical reason why they should not lapse. Jesus as enthroned "great high priest" is not only a lordly figure, distant from human involvement. Jesus was first a human who went through all that humans experience and suffer. He can "sympathize" with the depths of human problems, even while he is the exalted, heavenly priest. He did not succumb to failure in his temptations, but he certainly knows what those temptations are like and, it is implied, knows how such temptations can be overcome.

Believers can thus approach God with *confidence* (boldness). Such confidence results in mercy and grace "when they need it." The author here has in mind not the ultimate prayer for future salvation; he is thinking of the daily grind, when ordinary folk get into ordinary troubles (but ones that are problematic enough). Jesus as exalted high priest can help us surmount these problems because he has been through them himself.

Hebrews 5:7-9. This passage, closely related to the one above, is embedded in a structure that is comparing and contrasting the Jewish high priest with Jesus' role as high priest. In 4:15 Jesus is said to be able to sympathize with humans. In 5:2 the Jewish priest also has as one of his characteristics that he "is able to deal gently with the ignorant and wayward." Verses 7-9 then both pick up the theme expressed in 4:15 and serve as something of a comparison with 5:2. These verses, however, take the utility of Jesus' sufferings in a somewhat different direction.

In verses 7-8 it is commonly thought that a reference is being made to the Gethsemane tradition, but it is equally likely that the author has created an imaginative scenario. The author pictures Jesus' address to God in extreme terms ("loud cries and tears"—cf. the early gloss to Luke's Gethsemane story: 22:43-44). The clause in verse 7, "to the one who was able to save him from death," must mean that Jesus prayed to be saved from the *permanent* state of death. God hears him in granting him resurrection and exaltation.

The emphasis upon this agony does not lead, as in verse 15, to inspire confidence in believers that they have a sympathizing lord. Verse 8 moves toward affirming that the result of this agonizing was Jesus' "perfection." That is, his human suffering was the vehicle through which he was able to express fully his obedience. His full obedience in accepting death, despite its pain (cf. 12:2), *is* his "being made perfect"; and that perfection enables him to become the "cause," that is, source, effective agent, of the believer's "eternal salvation."

The designation of the believer as one "who obeys him" refers back to the obedience that Jesus learned. Salvation is a possibility for all believers who go through the same suffering-learning experiences as did Jesus when he faced death. While in 4:14-16 the human experience of Jesus leads to confidence in expecting daily needs to be met, in 5:7-9 the human suffering of Jesus elicits the believer's obedience learned through suffering, and through obedience to ultimate salvation.

Hebrews 10:16-25. In many ways this is a summary of much that has gone before in the sermon. Jeremiah 31 is cited again (first in 8:8-12).

Several phrases reappear that have already occurred in this week's readings from Hebrews.

It is indeed remarkable that it is only in Hebrews 8, out of the entire New Testament, that the citation by Jeremiah of a "new covenant" appears. The very notion that Christianity is a new covenant, a conception that has so often separated Judaism and Christianity into irreconcilable opposites, is also surprisingly rare in early Christianity.

The extent to which the author of Hebrews sees the new covenant (he uses the expression in 12:24) as replacing the "old" is widely disputed. That he uses the first covenant as a positive, if inadequate, base for his analogy suggests that his position is structurally ambiguous.

Perhaps the most provocative sentence in our text occurs in verse 18, after the citation of Jeremiah 31:34. "Where there is forgiveness of these ["lawless deeds"], there is no longer [a need for] any offering for sin." A striking and bold statement in almost any religious context! What can he mean? He implies, at least, that since the Christ event destroys the perpetuity of sinning, no future structure for sin-forgiveness is necessary. It is hard to imagine how any ecclesiastical system could avoid going against the meaning of this terse judgment!

The author's conviction that the death of Christ completely takes care of sin is here intensely expressed. This is true of the sins of the past; it also seems true of the sins of the future (except apostasy: cf. the immediately following section—10:26-31). This must mean that more than forgiveness occurs; it must also mean that the life of the believer is changed. *Confidence* not only implies assurance of forgiveness of the past; it is constitutive of a change of the self. It is a confidence that destroys the anxiety that leads to sin.

GOSPEL: JOHN 18:1—19:42

The Gospel reading for Good Friday contains John's entire story of Jesus' arrest, trial, execution, and burial. Like the Gospel reading for Passion Sunday (in that case Matthew), it is a long text, and I can only point to its main contours. As before it seems a wise judgment to emphasize the "plot" as John unfolds it, trying to ascertain what he wants the reader to "see" in the story. At the end of this description I will append a few observations comparing Matthew's version with that of John.

Arrest: 18:1-14.   John's story is in basic *structure* similar to that of Mark and Matthew. The *details* are frequently different. Sometimes these differences are insignificant variations; sometimes they point to important levels of meaning for the author.

John has no story of the prayer (although he has alluded to it in 12:27). The arresting officers now include the entire contingent of Roman soldiers in Jerusalem! John also adds that the Pharisees were involved. In John the disciples do not flee; Jesus bargains for their freedom. In John Jesus is taken first to the house of Annas, not to Caiaphas, who is the actual high priest.

Two significant moments in John's narrative occur in (a) the initial dialogue between Jesus and the authorities and (b) his rejoinder to Peter's act of violence. In the former (vv. 4-8a) Jesus takes the initiative and asks whom they are seeking. Then occurs one of the more remarkable scenes in the Gospel. Jesus replies to their response, "I am he." This is on the surface a simple acknowledgment that he is the Jesus they are looking for. But elsewhere in the Gospel this simple statement, "I am," points to an epiphany—the revelation of God through Jesus. When Jesus says these simple words, the arresting officials all react as if they are in the presence of the sacred: They fall to the ground. The question/answer is then repeated, and Jesus is arrested.

Here is a delicious moment, which would be easily handled by contemporary avant-garde filmmakers. The moment of epiphany and reverent response to it are inserted into the all-too-human story of arrest. The narrative then proceeds as if nothing unusual had happened. John is here writing for his readers, pointing out that at a deep level even Jesus' enemies have no choice but to do obeisance when the divine is present. Of course, on the story level they do have a choice, so they do arrest him. A filmmaker today might insert a one-second visual picture of the obeisance into the frames of the ordinary narrative.

The second significant sentence comes in Jesus' retort to Peter, after Peter has wounded the slave. "Am I not to drink the cup that the Father has given me?" (v. 11). Jesus is always in charge; Peter's attempt to resist arrest and defend Jesus is contrary to the divine plan that Jesus is carrying out (cf. also Matt. 26:52-54).

Peter's Denials and the Interrogation of Jesus: 18:15-27. John and Mark (followed by Matthew but *not* by Luke) agree in the interweaving of these, in themselves, separate stories. In verses 15-18, the entrance of Peter into the building in which the interrogation is taking place is described, along with the first denial. In verses 19-24 the interrogation itself is narrated. Verses 25-27 return to the scene with Peter, and include the second and third denials. Obviously the stories could have been told without the interweaving, as Luke chose to do. Thus the interweaving must be important for some reason other than historical reporting.

Verses 15-18. The location is, for some unexplained reason, not the house of the high priest Caiaphas but that of Annas, the influential patriarch of the family that had dominated the high priestly aristocracy for decades. The high priest was appointed and deposed by the Roman governor. Thus it was inevitable that this office carried political overtones. The very fact that Pilate kept Caiaphas in office during his entire term suggests that Caiaphas pleased him, that is, did things just as Pilate wished. This would mean, on the other hand, that Pilate could be equally beholden to Caiaphas, and the two doubtlessly played "I please you/you please me" games with each other.

Peter rejects any relationship with Jesus by a simple "I am not" in response to the first two questions. This is the negative counterpart to Jesus' affirmation in the arrest scene ("I am"), and it has been plausibly suggested that a contrast is being made here between Jesus' boldness in accepting the charge and Peter's cowardly denial.

Verses 19-24. John has little in common here with the Synoptics (Luke is perhaps closest). Most importantly, it is *not* a trial. A prisoner has been arrested, brought to the relevant officials, and initial interrogation occurs.

The questions asked of Jesus seem exactly what one would expect of a person suspected of some sort of insurrection—questions about teaching and followers. Jesus' response is summarized in verses 21-22, which in effect says: "My record is public; consult it." We learn nothing substantive here about charges or rebuttals (cf. by contrast the night trial in Mark). The scene seems to end at a standoff, and Annas sends Jesus to Caiaphas, who holds the official power.

The Gospel was written many decades after Jesus' day, and the tensions between the Johannine community and the synagogues "across the street" are sharp and apparent throughout the Gospel. If one transposes this scene of the interrogation of Jesus to conflictual encounters between members of the Johannine churches (which seem to have been largely Jewish) and the synagogues that opposed them, one can perhaps catch a "contemporary" flavor to this story. Does it teach the Johannine believers to make similar bold, noncommittal responses? This is one possibility to consider.

Verses 25-27. Now follows the terse conclusion of the story of Peter's denial. John is not interested in Peter's remorse. In John the story ends abruptly with the objective act. The important thing is what happened, not Peter's awareness of it.

Nevertheless, it is significant that John, Mark, and Matthew both interweave what happens to Jesus with what happens to Peter. This highlights the contrast between the responses: Jesus is bold (even, perhaps, in his silence); Peter is cowardly in his denials. It fits the consistently negative picture of Jesus' disciples at the time of his arrest and execution. *Only*

Jesus is the role model in the Gospels; even the most famous disciples are permitted no such place.

The Trial before Pilate: 18:28—19:16. Contrasted with the brief, inconclusive interrogation by Jewish officials, the Johannine Roman trial is a magnificently constructed drama in seven scenes. These scenes are demarcated by Pilate's movements inside and outside the Praetorium. The scenes inside all involve Jesus himself; two of them are dialogues between Pilate and Jesus, while the third is the scourging of Jesus by the Roman soldiers. The scenes can be outlined as follows:

1. *Outside.* Pilate and the Jewish authorities. *18:28-32.*
2. *Inside.* Pilate and Jesus debate kingship. *18:33-38a.*
3. *Outside.* Pilate and the Jews on Barabbas. *18:38b-40.*
4. *Inside.* Soldiers scourge and mock Jesus. *19:1-3.*
5. *Outside.* Pilate presents Jesus to Jews as a mock king. *19:4-7.*
6. *Inside.* Pilate and Jesus debate authority. *19:8-11.*
7. *Outside.* Pilate concedes to Jesus' execution. *19:12-16a.*

There is no space here to go into all of the interesting detail. One must comment, however, that this explicit dramatization (chap. 9 is a similar example) can be effectively presented by people taking parts and speaking the dialogue. This is one good way to avoid the potentially deadening monotony of reading such a long text as we have for Good Friday.

If we look at the "characters" in the drama, how would they be described? *Jesus* is silent before the Jews and the soldiers. He does speak freely with Pilate—and the discussions are surprisingly "philosophical." In scene 2 Pilate relates kingship to the usual standards of power. Jesus says that the true king is one who witnesses to truth (and that word is to be given its Greek notion of "ultimate reality"). In scene 6 the issue is authority. Pilate again understands authority simply from the normal definition of the power to dominate—this is the authority Pilate exercises. Jesus retorts that authority ultimately resides in the transcendent. Jesus and Pilate can only conflict with and misunderstand each other because they come from totally different worlds.

Pilate seems to be the urbane, haughty Roman, who ultimately has little commitment to anything but himself, and who is thus able to toy with the other actors and let the drama play out in transactions of power. Pilate seems disturbed by the possibility that Jesus might have some connection with divine power (19:8), but he is more influenced by the indirect threat of the Jewish leaders to accuse him before *his* authority, namely the emperor (19:12).

The Jewish authorities (the chief priests are the major actors here) are single-minded characters, aiming from beginning to end to have Jesus executed. This means they have to enlist Pilate on their side, since only he has the *ius gladius* (the right to execute). They badger him, threaten him, cajole him.

The trial is raucous. Only the two scenes between Jesus and Pilate contrast with a surprising serenity. The story clearly blames the Jews for Pilate's decision. Pilate's haughty cynicism, however, makes him into a less positive character than the description in Matthew. Pilate remains aloof to the very end. "Shall I crucify your King?" he ironically asks. "Then he handed him over to them [in the context the antecedent has to be the chief priests] to be crucified." Pilate has capitulated and therefore incurred culpability along with the high priests.

The Crucifixion: 19:16b-37.   Nothing shows more clearly the dangers to interpretation that the harmonization of the Gospels causes than reading John's story of the crucifixion. Obviously a few basic things remain the same. Jesus is crucified with two other criminals. An inscription on the cross identifies Jesus as "King of the Jews." Reference to the dividing of Jesus' clothing and the offering of some drink (in allusion to Psalms 22 and 69) and the statement that Jesus died round out the agreements between John and the Synoptics.

How much is different! First, what is absent from John: Simon of Cyrene, the mocking of Jesus (by people, priests, and criminals), the hour scheme, the references to darkness and the rending of the temple curtain, the acclamation by the Roman soldier(s). These details that so color our presentation of and feeling for the story are missing.

What do we find instead? First, Jesus carries his own cross. Any suggestion that he is weak is thus removed. If one were filling in details from what the Gospel has previously told us, we would rather suppose that he strides confidently carrying the weight as if it were nothing.

The reference to the inscription is enlarged and Pilate is brought into the picture one last time. The inscription is written in three languages, as befits royalty, and Pilate refuses to alter it to fit Jewish sensitivities. Pilate has finally acknowledged (if without intending it) who Jesus really is, as contrasted with the obdurate Jewish authorities.

The tradition about the clothes is given more prominence, and the Psalm verse (22:18) is explicitly cited. Whether the seamless garment has an added symbolism has been vigorously argued by scholars with inconclusive results.

The most startling addition is the scene with Jesus' mother and the beloved disciple. It is obvious that the author is communicating something he considers important. The scene must be symbolic, since the author elsewhere shows no interest in historical details. It is Jesus' last action, and its occurrence brings the notice that Jesus knew that all was "finished," that is, completed (v. 28). So in some way the handing over of mother to disciple seems to symbolize an important, final act of the earthly Jesus.

Alas, just what the symbolic meaning is cannot be reconstructed with any confidence. Many different suggestions have been made, but none has convinced the majority of interpreters. Jesus' mother has not appeared since the wedding at Cana, where she is not given a very positive role. What does she stand for here? And who *is* the beloved disciple? Scholars have not come close to agreeing on any identification. In some sense he has to represent the ideal believer. After all, he is the one who in the plot is the first truly to believe (20:8). Does the mother stand for Jewish Christianity, while the disciple represents Gentile? Does she represent the timid believer, while he, the robust?

All it is possible to say here is that the scene is Jesus' final act *with regard to the community*. The act seems to be one of unification—the bringing together of disparate elements. The theme of unity—or desired unity—surfaces explicitly at the end of the "high-priestly prayer" (17:20-23). Beyond that, the event, because of our ignorance, will always remain enigmatic and mysterious, and it is wise not to be too certain that we know exactly what it means.

John has his own final word of Jesus: "It is perfected [or finished or completed]." It is perfected in the sense that Jesus has perfectly carried out God's will in his mission on earth. The scene also elaborately pictures the soldiers' acts of brutality, acts that are so closely tied to the fulfillment of Scripture that they may most simply be seen as details spun out of reflection on these passages. The emission of water and blood has been interpreted by many as a symbol for the relation of the sacraments to Jesus' death.

John's portrayal is not surprising, once one considers that Jesus in all events in his earthly life is completely in control, acting out, even provoking what happens because it is all a divine design for the salvation of the world. Yes, Jesus is human, but he is so aligned with God's will that he confidently marches through all the events, including the final one of death by crucifixion, with confidence and serenity. He dies in perfect control because his will is perfectly subordinated to that of his Father (cf. 5:30).

The Burial: 19:38-42. The stark account of the burial in Mark, in which Jesus is hastily laid in a tomb by a nondisciple before the Sabbath begins, has been softened by all the other accounts. John's account is the most elaborate, and in it Jesus' body receives all the necessary preparations for burial.

As in Matthew, Joseph is a disciple. John adds Nicodemus, not exactly named as a disciple but certainly a sympathizer (cf. 7:50-52). Nicodemus is obviously rich and is willing to use his wealth to prepare Jesus for burial. The amount of spices (about seventy-five pounds) is, of course, extravagant, and certainly points to some symbolic meaning. It has been plausibly suggested that, since royal figures at their burial sometimes had huge amounts of spices placed in the tomb, Jesus is buried, just as he is crucified, as a king.

Comparison between Matthew and John.   The main difference may lie in the different perspectives of Jesus given by the Evangelists—differences, of course, that go back to basic christological judgments.

For Matthew, Jesus is the Son of God-Messiah. Yet he is perceived as completely human and he thus can function as an example of faithful human suffering. The Jesus facing death has recognizable human uncertainties: the Gethsemane scene, the beating that rendered him unable to do what most criminals are made to do (i.e., carry his own cross), the cry of forsakenness. Jesus is the man of faith who must overcome doubt and apparent meaninglessness to maintain that faith.

For John, Jesus is also human, is flesh. Yet there is a certainty that Jesus possesses of his "origin"—his place with the Father—that enables him to walk above the ordinary anxieties of humans facing death. He sweeps aside the Gethsemane scene with one allusion (12:27). He engages in theological dialogue with the official who holds the decision for life or death in his hand, he strides confidently carrying the cross to his death, he utters, not a cry of abandonment, but one of fulfillment at the end. It is true that John calls the disciples to a love which imitates the self-giving of Jesus (12:24-26); but it is hard to imagine an ordinary human facing death with the lordly serenity that John's Jesus does.

It is really not at all appropriate to bring Chalcedon to bear on this difference, with its struggle to find the right way of saying that Jesus is both divine and human. And yet the temptation to do so suggests that Chalcedon is somehow rooted in the different portrayals of Jesus in the New Testament. Jesus is human, so we can understand his agony and use him as an example. Jesus is divine, so we can look thankfully at what God has done for us that we cannot do for ourselves—or imitate. "It is completed." Matthew gives us a Jesus related to a humanity we know all too well. John gives us a Jesus whose humanity is a majestic disclosure of God's sovereign beneficence to us and in us.

HOMILETICAL REFLECTIONS

To look back intellectually and emotionally over the texts for all of Holy Week overwhelms one with a kind of spiritual vertigo. Some of us have spent a lifetime trying to come to terms with these texts, and we may feel we have only just begun to allow the challenges in them to be heard.

Just what is it about these texts that is so difficult, so provocative, so conducive to flight, and yet so moving and meaningful? Is it that we do not like to suffer? Yes, we fear pain, but for a cause we *really believe in*, we will accept pain.

Is it the stern call to obedience (which may lead to suffering but is never to be equated with it)? Yes, obedience so often seems drudgery. Yet most of us experience genuine obedience to something we *really believe in*. We are obedient to our work, to our family, to our social obligations, even to service in the community, local or global. It is not foreign to us to say, "I *must* do this for. . . ."

What is it then that holds us from wholehearted commitment to the story of Jesus? It may just be that the dangerous threat to ourselves we dimly or urgently feel in these texts is the haunting sense that we are living, with all our readiness to be obedient and to suffer, in a false reality. We go to church, we participate in its activities, we have obligations in our intimate circle of loved ones, we give time and energy and money to social concerns, we acknowledge the moral and stern beauty of the passion story. But all these can have their place in a false world, where even religion conceals the sham.

If then we already live in a pious and moral world, what is the source of our discomfort? Is it that we do not try hard enough? Or is it perhaps that we try too hard and yet attain little peace? Is it perhaps that the true world out of which the Jesus story lives and has its power is first of all a world of gift, not demand? Obedience based on self-forgetful care for others, not on command? Suffering accepted as expression of the power of love, not masochistic self-centeredness?

What makes us want to flee from these texts is then the alternate world they propose, a world so different from the pious and polite world in which we have our grim comfort, accompanied with little ecstasy. In the new world God is the self-giving One, and our selves are anchored in the richness of that gift. *That* is the real difference. God gives and we are empowered to live richly, to forget ourselves, our anxieties, our senses of duty and to plunge joyfully into the service now made possible by that gift. And out of this gift we are made whole and can live authentically in the ecstasy and power of self-giving.

The story of Jesus is then paradigm for us, because that story presents one who by his self-forgetfulness showed perfect awareness of the gift of

God and therefore perfect service. In this sense he is the "pioneer and perfecter of our faith" (Heb. 12:2). The story of Jesus calls us *really to believe in* that God and thus really to live in the world of the Jesus story. Do we dare have the confidence of such belief?

The world, of course, sees Christian service and suffering as obeisance to a god of weakness and stupidity. To take up these texts and follow them is to risk entering an alternate world in which wisdom and power are radically redefined. It is to this world that the Christian story invites us. It cannot prove that its world is true. But the joyful confession of believers throughout the centuries is that it *is* the true world. God gives life unsparingly and calls us to that same joyful risk in our self-understandings and in our relations with our neighbors.